BRITISH SEA POWER
IN THE 1980s

BRITISH SEA POWER
IN THE 1980s

REAR ADMIRAL J.R.HILL

LONDON

IAN ALLAN LTD

First published 1985

ISBN 0 7110 1473 6

Published by Ian Allan Ltd, Shepperton, Surrey;
and printed by Ian Allan Printing Ltd at their works
at Coombelands in Runnymede, England.

Design: C. Botwright.

Below:
A combined NATO force in the Mediterranean.
NATO photograph

Contents

Preface

This book began as a second edition of *The Royal Navy Today and Tomorrow*, which was first published in November 1981. But it quickly became apparent that it should be regarded as a new project and given a new title. There were two good reasons for this. First, the intervening three years were unusually crowded. The reductions in Britain's maritime strength announced in the White Paper 'Defence: The Way Forward' (Cmnd 8288), in June 1981, had fortunately had insufficient time to take full effect when the South Atlantic conflict erupted in April 1982. At the successful conclusion of that conflict there was good reason for reassessment of every aspect of British sea power, from the smallest material detail to the fundamental elements of strategy. There was no shortage of radical propositions for the future; nor was there any shortage, particularly in Whitehall, of arguments that the Falklands was a non-recurring phenomenon and that the previous decisions should stand. No book about the British maritime scene in the 1980s can avoid entering that debate.

Secondly, my own position has changed. In 1981 I was still a serving officer, and however many disclaimers such an officer makes about expressing his own opinions and not those of the government, he must confine his comments in a way that will not involve him in a head-on public clash with government policy. Lord Chatfield in 1933 put it this way:

We do not lay down policy – we are the national instrument for carrying it out . . . we are responsible for giving correct advice as to our needs. We have no wish to say more; it would be neglecting our constitutional duty to say less.

However, having now been on the retired list for two years, I am much more free to express opinions on the full range of policy and to put forward, in this book, views of my own on both material and strategic matters. I do not pretend in a script of 40,000 words to have made a comprehensive exposition of either, but there may be enough ideas here to enliven debate.

It is important to the maritime health of this country that debate should continue. There are, as I have said, plenty of people in and close to government whose predisposition towards the largely continental and almost entirely alliance-dependent 'strategy', developed in the late 1960s and 1970s and reaching its extreme in Cmnd 8288, is largely undented. They could, in my view – and I am sure in the view of much of the public – do with a good deal more prodding. Perhaps there is a broomhandle or two in this book.

Naturally not all the material is new. It would be odd if two books by the same person on such similar subjects within four years had entirely different pictures or wording. So I have tried to keep the best of the relevant material from *The Royal Navy Today and Tomorrow* while offering enough that is new, both visually and in ideas, to live up to the book's name.

It is a more personal document than *The Royal Navy Today and Tomorrow*. But I must acknowledge in particular the help of two groups of people. The first was the core of a seminar that gathered twice at Gosport in the early 1980s under the rubric of 'Medium Maritime Power': Dr Clive Archer, Sir James Cable, Adm Sir James Eberle, Rear Adm Edward Gueritz, Vice Adm Sir Ian McGeoch, Professors Peter Nailor and Bryan Ranft, Michael Ranken, Geoffrey Till and Elizabeth Young. They sharpened and tempered such blunt ideas as I had on this central subject. The second was more diverse and its help more material: among them Maj Alastair Donald, Capt Jim Flindell, Second Officer Melville-Brown, Capt Derek Oakley, Mr Lawrence Phillips, Cdr Francis Ponsonby, CPO Smart, Mr Speakman, Capt Ian Sutherland, Second Officer Moira Tate and Capt Tony Wigley. Along with firms such as British Shipbuilders, Marconi, Ocean Containers Ltd, Plessey, Rolls-Royce and Westland, they provided most of the new visual material. My thanks are due to them all: and finally to my wife who, as ever, not only typed the manuscript but cast a cool eye over its more obscure passages. No one demonstrates better that there is more to logic than arguments, and more to mathematics than adding up.

J. R. Hill

1 A Definition, and some History

Sea power is the ability to use the sea. That is the most terse of all the available definitions but also the most satisfying, because like a pithy musical statement at the start of a sonata it is capable of intense and logical development.

Instantly the question is raised: To what uses shall the sea be put? The answers come thick and fast. First, security: a nation-state will always prefer to conduct its defence at a distance from its own territory. Second, trade: few nations can flourish in self-sufficiency, and the sea has always been a major trade route for most. Third, resource enjoyment: the sea offers riches in both living and non-living forms, and their exploitation can account for a sizeable proportion of national wealth. Fourth, recreation and well being: a concern of the sophisticated perhaps, but by no means a negligible factor. And, finally, because it springs from the effective exercise of the other uses, political and diplomatic influence: the extra lever that can persuade or coerce in the complicated conduct of international affairs.

An island state is bound to look at sea power in all these ways, even if it does not choose to take up some of the options. In fact Britain has throughout most of its past given attention to most of them and can plausibly be put forward as the prime example in history of a nation which has been able to deploy integrated, far-reaching maritime power.

Below:
In medieval sea fighting, ships were used as infantry carriers. In this battle (La Rochelle, 1372) the English were defeated.
National Maritime Museum

This book will not be able to follow all the strands of that thick, complex network. It can do no more than keep in mind the economic elements of sea power – the merchant marine and the trading and financial complex that backs it; the fisheries and their secondary industries; the offshore extractive industries and their multinational ramifications; the recreational uses – and concentrate on the organisations that ensure the security of the state, the protection of trade, and the continuance of good order, at sea: the Royal Navy, the maritime element of the Royal Air Force, and the ancillary forces that support them.

Some History

Security against invasion certainly dominated the early requirement for a British Navy. There were plenty of threats: Danes, Norsemen, Saxons, Normans, and later France and Spain. Strong rulers who appreciated the importance of defending the sea approaches, like Alfred and Elizabeth I, succeeded in preventing invasion; one who did not was Harold Godwinson, who failed and paid with his kingdom and his life.

The general pattern of the Navy up to the 16th century was a nucleus of a few King's Ships, joined in time of need by a sort of maritime *levée en masse*. This was made easier by the fact that merchant and war vessels were not sharply differentiated, their main function in war being to carry soldiers and their main fighting method being boarding.

The 16th century was a time of transition and expansion. Improvements in navigation and sailing abilities and skills gave opportunities for widespread ocean voyaging. Developments in shipbuilding allowed large cannon to be mounted in a ship's broadside; this changed the nature of sea-fighting, making it more specialised and professional, and there was more differentiation between merchant and military vessels. To be sure, merchant ships still commonly had to fight their way into trading patterns against Spanish or Portuguese claims to monopoly, so their armaments were not negligible. The consequence of all these developments was an extremely flexible maritime organisation, which was proved by the 'ad hoc' triumph against the Spanish Armada, in which 34 royal ships were joined by over 100 merchant ships and had already inflicted, by harrying, fire and battery, a signal defeat on the Spanish ships before the gale blew and they were scattered.

Under the early Stuarts British maritime policy was in danger of losing its way. Charles I's closed-sea doctrine was singularly inward-looking and inappropriate to the time. But it was corrected by Cromwell's Western Design, which turned British policy towards gaining 'an interest in that part of the West Indies in the possession of the Spaniards' and at the same time challenged Dutch trade expansion. In the three Dutch wars that followed there was much hard fighting and the eventual British success sprang more from a broader economic base and powerful allies than from any preponderance of skill.

During this period the Royal Navy as we know it took shape. It was now recognisably a permanent national force.

Actions were fought by specialised fighting ships; merchant ships fought only in self defence, and in dangerous waters they expected to be convoyed. Warship design was standardised and tactics formalised: now that the great gun mounted in the broadside was the primary weapon at sea, the line of battle became the accepted fighting formation. Finally, in this era of ordering and organisation, the Navy found its procurement, provisioning, pay, officer structure and secretarial practices reformed by Samuel Pepys. By the time he left office in 1659 it was a well-ordered and professional force and its administration rested on a sound basis.

The foundations were now laid for the classical course of British policy: ensuring that no continental power dominated Europe, and concurrently expanding overseas trade and possessions. Inevitably this led to conflict with France, the major European power, and from 1690 to 1815 France was a consistent opponent in a series of wars in which the other participants changed sides frequently.

This was on the whole an immensely successful period for the Royal Navy. There was some governmental neglect in time of peace, and in war there were some checks and reverses, mostly caused by too slavish a following of the line-of-battle doctrine or inadequate preparation for amphibious operations; but in general the course of events led steadily towards the establishment of maritime dominance which was certainly achieved by the first decade of the 19th century.

Life in the Navy in this classical age was in many aspects harsh and dangerous. The officers had reasonable if cramped conditions and could put together considerable fortunes in prize money if they were lucky; the ratings, more than half of them conscripted by the rough and ready mechanism of the press gang, lived by their guns in crowded and unhealthy conditions, feeding when at sea on salt beef and biscuit and precious little else except rum. Discipline was by modern standards brutal. But then, whatever its art may suggest, the 18th century was not a pretty age ashore or afloat; and there is ample evidence that in most ships, care and concern by officers for the men, shared danger and professional pride formed the true core of discipline, whatever its outward rigours. Opponents might show skill and elan, and sometimes have better equipment; but the British always excelled in one quality: tenacity. Harnessed by commanders with offensive flair, this quality led to great victories. In the hands of lesser men it just meant not losing, holding what had been gained, protecting the trade which went on, war or no war.

It was the Navy's golden age, and like all such ages produced more than its share of famous men. Rooke, Anson the circumnavigator and administrator, Hawke who won at Quiberon Bay in a shrieking gale, Boscawen and Rodney; then in the Napoleonic wars such a cluster that one wonders which

to choose: Barham the strategist, Jervis of St Vincent, Duncan of Camperdown, Howe of the First of June, Cornwallis and Collingwood the blockade specialists, Saumarez and Pellew. But of all the great names of this age two can be selected for special mention: James Cook and Horatio Nelson.

Cook came to the Navy as a lower-deck volunteer after serving in North Sea colliers. By sheer ability he rose through the rank of master (or navigator) to commander to captain; and in the course of this he carried out his three great voyages of discovery to the Pacific. He set standards in the accuracy of hydrographic surveying that have endured to the present day. His enterprise and spirit of scientific enquiry were matched by consistency of purpose. His care for his ships' companies' conditions and hygiene was so good that in his first voyage not a man died from scurvy. The man and his work were universally admired and respected; the French Navy was instructed not to molest him.

Nelson's upbringing in a county parsonage was modest. He had influential relations who helped his advancement, but not so much as did his ability, his swift appreciation of problems, and more than anything his ardour for battle and glory. As commodore and admiral his success in battle was unparalleled and protean: his brilliant and brave manoeuvre at St Vincent, his cool seizure of an opportunity for annihilation (a favourite word of his) at the Nile, his gutsy slogging-match at Copenhagen – not to mention his diplomacy after it – his vigil on the prolonged and wearing blockade of Toulon, and the culmination of it all at Trafalgar, showed him as a master of all the maritime arts. He was vain, ebullient, full of human foibles and frailties; the Fleet loved him for them almost as much as for his courage and skill.

These two men, Cook and Nelson, were about as different in character as it is possible to conceive. Yet the Royal Navy accommodated them both, even though neither was in its classic mould. And they shared qualities which, as intelligent men, they had learnt from naval service: a vast and comprehensive professionalism; immense attention to detail; and constant care for the men under their command. Those lessons are re-learnt by every generation of naval officer, then, today and tomorrow.

In the 19th century the Royal Navy was pre-eminent, the instrument of Pax Britannica, and one of the chief motors of Empire. Its problems concerned new technological, administrative and social practices more than fighting mortal enemies. Technically, it moved in well under a century from wood and sail and cannonballs to steel and steam and shells. Administratively, it reformed many of its practices and much improved living and working conditions. There were some setbacks and some foot-dragging but in general the changes were accomplished; the only question that arose, in the face of a growing challenge from Germany, was whether they had been fast enough.

One man who did not think so was Adm 'Jacky' Fisher, a character several times larger than life. His rationalisations between 1900 and 1910 shook down the Navy into a balanced, very powerful battle fleet with the bulk of other naval forces structured to meet that fleet's purposes. Conceptually it owed much to the American Adm Mahan's theories of sea power, particularly on the pre-eminence of fleet action in establishing command of the sea, and it was technically derivative too. But its organisation and structure were Fisher's own, and its mission clear: to counter the German High Seas Fleet and defeat it if it ventured to break out from its bases. The defects were of Fisher's making too: over-centralisation of command

and control, unwillingness of subordinates to take initiatives, and a tendency to cliqueyness and intrigue.

In World War 1 the Fleet's only action at Jutland ended in the outnumbered Germans returning to their base with little loss. If the British under Jellicoe did not win, they certainly did not lose; and the High Seas Fleet did not seek battle again. But the guns at Jutland, newly in action though they were, sounded the finale of the great battles between lines of ships. They were already giving place to two new elements of maritime warfare; the submarine and aircraft.

Some elements in Germany, seeing her as likely to remain the weaker naval power, had always been drawn towards attacking Allied commerce – the classical *guerre de course*. After many false starts owing to misgivings about an adverse American reaction (which turned out to be well justified), the Germans settled on unrestricted submarine warfare in early 1917. It posed a very severe threat to Britain, and the institution of mercantile convoys from mid-1917 came only just in time. Both submarine and anti-submarine methods were still fairly crude, with much use of surface gunfire – partly, in

Right:
The old order and the new: submarines passing HMS *Dreadnought*, 1906. *National Maritime Museum*

Below:
The development of naval aviation was the chief innovation in the Fleet between the wars. Fairey IIIFs over HMS *Courageous* in the Mediterranean. *Imperial War Museum*

the case of the submarines, to conserve torpedoes – and the concentration of merchant ships with some sort of escort was enough to defeat the submarines even though underwater detection was in its infancy.

As for aircraft, their maritime roles in World War 1 involved a good deal of scouting and reconnaissance, with limited offensive operations mounted from shore bases. It was between the wars that their potential for shipborne operations was developed, not so fully by the Royal Navy as by the United States. Nor, indeed, was their use for anti-submarine work so well exploited as it might have been; the Navy had too much confidence in shipborne systems, and Coastal Command of the newly-formed Royal Air Force had low priority in a time of restricted finance.

Financial stringency was relaxed only just in time to allow the Navy to enter World War 2 in reasonable shape. It had owed much in the 1930s to Admiral of the Fleet Lord Chatfield's management and leadership; he may have over-emphasised battleship construction, but his programmes

ensured that the hard core existed of a fighting service facing one of its greatest challenges. In fact the Royal Navy in World War 2 was very much an all-arms maritime force and it is notable how few campaigns or even actions were waged by forces of one kind alone. The aircraft was a necessary component of the great majority of maritime operations, from fleet action to the titanic struggle in the Atlantic against the U-boats. Submarines of the Royal Navy were not closely integrated into such operations but were a critical factor in many campaigns. Surface units were ubiquitous. And sea power reached what is perhaps its high point so far in the great

Below:
Defeat of the U-boats in the Atlantic: an indisputably vital victory for British sea power in both world wars. *HMS Vernon*

Bottom:
HMS *Ark Royal* in the 1970s. *Crown Copyright*

amphibious operations in all theatres of war, from Madagascar to Normandy to Iwo Jima. Throughout this period, and it is not the least astonishing of the achievements, the Navy was conducting a technical revolution as it entered the electronic age with radar, radio direction-finding, voice radio, cryptography and code-breaking, and new sonic systems.

It ended World War 2 as a very successful service. It had fought and won one vital battle in the Atlantic, and many more of the first importance. It had proved itself capable of nearly tenfold expansion (its wartime strength was 863,500) and great feats of organisation in the naval control of shipping and mounting of amphibious operations. Most of all it had proved over and over again its courage and tenacity.

It now had to move into a rapidly changing, difficult and still dangerous world. With resources that were in any case limited and diminished with the relative worsening of the country's economic health, with shrinking imperial commitments and expanding alliance concerns, and above all with the realities of the atomic age and the existence of Superpowers: with all these it had to come to terms. It had to convince sceptics and scoffers that it still had a role; sometimes, even, it seemed it had to convince itself. Often, as it struggled to maintain a balanced force that would be an instrument of sea power appropriate to the nation and the time, its leaders would remind their questioners of the need to deal with the unforeseen. Just how far from prediction the unforeseen can be was shown by the events of 1982 in the South Atlantic, and they point a cautionary lesson to professional and layman alike as those events too recede into history.

12

Above:
The next generation of seaborne air power: A VSTOL Sea Harrier gets airborne during the South Atlantic conflict, 1982. *Crown Copyright*

Below:
Sea power got them there: British troops restore the Union flag to the Falklands. *Crown Copyright*

2 The Task

There is no single, authoritative, detailed statement of the task that the Royal Navy is intended to fulfil. It is possible though to derive from Defence White Papers and the statements of senior officers and officials a reasonable summary of the current orthodoxy. It is also possible, and has increasingly become so, to detect in these statements (as well as in writings that come from places less close to Whitehall) some of the tensions in and challenges to that orthodoxy. Therefore this chapter will fall into two parts: first, what may be called the official line; second, the main strands of an alternative view.

The Official Line

As a sovereign nation Britain has the ultimate responsibility for its own security. But in a world where superpowers and power groupings exist, she has judged that she cannot fulfil that responsibility from her resources alone. She has therefore chosen to belong to an alliance, the North Atlantic Treaty Organisation (NATO), which provides mutual support and, critically, engages the United States of America in the defence of Western Europe.

Because NATO is so important to Britain, British forces must be compatible with NATO's strategy and must make an appropriate contribution to the alliance. All major projects for new equipments and formations have for many years had to be justified against these criteria. NATO strategy has since the

late 1960s rested on the concept of flexible response: the ability to respond to every threat or use of force at an appropriate level and to pose to the opponent a credible counter-threat of escalation. Thus confronted, a rational opponent will see that no use of force is possible without the ultimate risk to himself either of unacceptable damage or of climbing down; and he will consequently be deterred from embarking on coercive action in the first place.

In judging Britain's contribution to the NATO forces implementing this strategy, account must be taken of many factors: her written commitment to keep troops and an air force on the continent of Europe, her economic and human resources, her geo-strategic position within the alliance and her special skills and expertise in certain kinds of military activity. In consequence successive governments have evolved a defence structure resting on four pillars: an independent element of strategic and theatre nuclear forces committed to the alliance; the direct defence of the United Kingdom homeland; a major land and air contribution on the European mainland; and a major maritime effort in the Eastern Atlantic and Channel. There are two further roles that in large part make use of the forces provided for the four primary ones: reinforcement in certain contingencies of the flanks of NATO; and meeting, outside the NATO area, both specific British responsibilities and the growing importance to the West of supporting our friends and contributing to world stability.

British maritime forces are involved in all these roles: in the case of the continental commitment the task is a supporting one, but nevertheless vital, since to sustain a NATO campaign in Central Europe and bring it to a successful conclusion, reinforcement and resupply by sea across the Atlantic and Channel are necessary. For the other roles the involvement is direct.

Nuclear Deterrence is the higher end of the escalatory ladder, but in the doctrine of flexible response it covers not just one step but several. The highest of all is a strategic second-strike capability, able in all circumstances to inflict unacceptable damage on the homeland of an aggressor. Britain's strategic deterrent, which is sea-based in ballistic missile submarines and was laid down by the then Government in 1981 as the Royal Navy's first and most vital task, is committed to the alliance, but its control remains entirely in British hands. This factor in the nuclear balance would compel any potential attacker to regard the risks of aggression in Europe as very grave, whatever his reading of the strength of the American nuclear commitment. This 'second centre of nuclear decision making' has been a valued feature of NATO deterrence for many years.

Strategic nuclear forces are, in broad terms, relatively cheap to run but expensive to replace, and because financial provision for a replacement of the present Polaris force was deferred during the 1970s, the financial commitment bears more heavily on the rest of the defence programme now the decision to replace has been made.

Below:
The NATO flag is paraded with those of some NATO nations during a port visit by the Standing Naval Force, Channel.
Crown Copyright

Above:
Britain's independent strategic nuclear deterrent is at present carried in four submarines like HMS *Resolution*, pictured here.
Crown Copyright

Below:
A Soviet ballistic missile submarine of the 'Delta' class.
Crown Copyright

Bottom:
Air surveillance off the coast of Scotland. An RAF Nimrod in attendance on a Soviet 'Echo-II' class submarine, just one element of the Soviet threat to the NATO Atlantic Strike Fleet.
Crown Copyright

Theatre nuclear weapons in the maritime field can justly be described as tactical. There are many circumstances in modern sea-fighting where a nuclear warhead's extra destructive power can compensate for lack of accuracy, and the Soviet Union – which is clearly the threat with which NATO is primarily concerned – is known to have extensive stocks for a wide range of weapons. If the West was to forego similar advantages the Soviets would be given a free ride. Therefore, in spite of the certainty that political constraints on use would be severe – and, in the initial stages of a non-nuclear conflict, total – British maritime forces need a tactical nuclear capability.

The Defence of the UK Base is important not only for the preservation of territorial integrity but to NATO as a whole, since Britain's geographical position provides a forward base for operations in the Atlantic, a main base for operations in the Channel and North Sea and a rear base for operations on the Continent. Critical to these functions is the continued operation of the ports, and this demands from the Royal Navy an extensive mine countermeasures effort. Air and sea surveillance is also required against the possibility of clandestine operations or more overt raids.

In these days of extensive exploitation of offshore resources, the UK home economic base extends far offshore, to the oil and gas fields of the North Sea and the fisheries round the coast, and the commitment to its protection applies both in peace and war. This demands air and sea forces for patrol, surveillance and regulatory action; they need not be of highly warlike nature – indeed it is better for peacetime work if they are limited in this regard – but they do need to be capable of all-weather operation and numerous enough to be an effective constabulary.

The Eastern Atlantic and Channel is the area which demands most from Britain's maritime forces in terms of war-fighting strength. Its importance to any Atlantic alliance, where the main threat comes from the eastern side of the continent of Europe and the main power base is in the USA across 3,000 miles of ocean, is self-evident. The requirement for Britain, with its special skills, immense experience and crucial geographical position, to make a major contribution is generally accepted. The threat comes mainly from the Soviet Northern Fleet, a very modern, powerful and numerous force whose greatest strength lies in its 150 submarines (over half of them nuclear-powered), 75 major surface combatants and 100 long-range land-based aircraft. There is great emphasis on long-range anti-ship missile capability and on co-ordinated operations. Against this threat the British maritime forces' task can be split into several elements.

First is the containment of Soviet naval forces. Geography has conferred an advantage to NATO in the 'choke points' of the Greenland-Iceland-UK gap, through which Soviet Northern Fleet units would have to pass to reach the Atlantic proper. NATO (and until the arrival of US forces, this means mainly British) units, particularly submarines and long-range maritime patrol aircraft, would seek to hinder such deployments.

Second, the UK contribution to the anti-submarine defence of the US Strike Fleet Atlantic is designed to allow the US strike carriers to concentrate on their air defence and strike/attack roles. British forces would make up Anti-Submarine Group 2 comprising one or two anti-submarine carriers with Sea Harriers and anti-submarine helicopters, destroyers and frigates, long-range maritime patrol aircraft and perhaps nuclear-powered attack submarines.

Third, the UK has to make a contribution to the direct defence of reinforcement and resupply shipping crossing the Atlantic. This would be essential to counter opposing forces which had been in position before hostilities began or had found their way through the choke points in spite of NATO's containment operations. For such a protection-of-shipping task, extending as it does to over 1,000 cargoes a month, numerous surface escorts and considerable air support are required.

Finally, the approaches to the United Kingdom and the Channel crossings cannot be left to themselves. Organisation of shipping and the physical means of administering it will require a considerable effort; defence against possible attack will require much more. Clearly all the patrol craft used in peacetime, as well as some shore-based air resources, will need to be available here.

But the most sophisticated and therefore most costly effort has to go into the first three elements, and it is the balance between these that was reviewed by the then Government in 1980-81, with results published in a document called 'The Way Forward' in June 1981. In this, arguing that the power of maritime air systems and submarines was increasing and that of surface ships relatively declining, the Secretary of State for Defence, Mr (now Sir) John Nott, stated that:

'. . . for the future the most cost-effective maritime mix – the best-balanced operational contribution for our situation – will be one which continues to enhance our maritime-air and submarine effort, but accepts a reduction below current plans

Left:
A conventionally-powered Soviet submarine of the 'Foxtrot' class. *Crown Copyright*

Below:
A Soviet 'Krivak' class frigate observed by HMS *Rhyl*. *Crown Copyright*

in the size of our surface fleet and the scale and sophistication of new ship-building, and breaks away from the practice of costly mid-life modernisation.'

This decision implied greater emphasis on the first – containment – element of the task and less on the other two. It caused great controversy, which will be addressed later in the chapter.

Above:
An example of widening Soviet maritime horizons: the Soviet carrier *Novorossiysk*. In 1984 there were four of this class in the Soviet Navy. *Crown Copyright*

Below:
Amphibious forces to help protect NATO's northern flank are provided by the Royal Marines, and by the Royal Netherlands Marine Corps, pictured here preparing to embark in RN helicopters. *Crown Copyright*

The Deployment of Amphibious Forces is a specialist task applicable particularly, in the case of British forces, to the Northern Flank of NATO. It demands specially-trained infantry and supporting arms, suitable shipping to carry them and the necessary protection for them at sea. Because northern Norway in particular is much closer to Russia than it is to UK; because one Norwegian brigade faces seven Soviet divisions in peacetime; and because other Russian concerns in the Norwegian Sea, including the deployment of ballistic missile submarines, are regarded by them as very important, this task might assume vast proportions unless it could be completed before the outbreak of hostilities.

The Support of Wider Defence Interests is a task that is national in execution, even if its intention and effects are to benefit the West generally. It is necessary for several reasons: the expansion of Soviet influence, which by its nature is inimical to Western interests; the instability of the political situation in many parts of the world; claims by some nations to jurisdiction which is unjustified by international law; and

commitments which can be called the 'residue of empire'.

The task can be carried out at three levels: defence aid in the form of equipment sales, loan personnel, training and advice; periodic deployment of British forces for exercises, visits and training; and the ability to deploy forces for deterrent or defensive action where circumstances make this necessary in the last resort. At the first of these levels, naval participation is a function not only of British expertise but also of success in designing naval equipment that is attractive to foreign customers. At the second and third, naval participation is essential, and in the very nature of geography tends to be predominant. Up to about 1980, because British naval forces had been comprehensive in operational scope and ocean-going in character, the requirement could be met from NATO-committed units. The loss of fixed-wing aircraft carriers diminished autonomy and limited the options; the reductions in the surface fleet consequent on 'The Way Forward' would have sharpened this process greatly. Thus the South Atlantic campaign of 1982, with its requirement to carry out operations of a scale long since discounted by government plans, posed the severest of challenges. The Royal Navy's high standards of training, resource and tenacity, with a little bit of luck, carried its part of the operation through.

Examples of NATO Exercises and Co-operation

Above right:
The Standing Naval Force, Channel.
Crown Copyright

Right:
The Naval On-call Force, Mediterranean. *NATO photograph*

Below:
A British tanker fuels a Turkish and an American destroyer.
NATO photograph

Alternative Views

It would be surprising if, in a democracy, there were not a good many people who dissented from the official line. It would be even more surprising if such people put forward a unanimously agreed alternative policy. But since the late 1970s there has been forming a coherent view held by a significant proportion of the dissenters, and it is this that I shall try to summarise. First, however, let us look very briefly at three extreme forms of dissent that are not in the main stream.

The first is nuclear pacifism, rejecting the British independent deterrent, a nuclear tactical capability, and US bases in Britain. This is sometimes put forward as a way of releasing funds for a strong conventional Royal Navy, but in the political climate that such a policy would imply, it quite simply would not. It would lead instead to a weak, neutral-leaning Britain with a navy reduced to a coast defence force.

The second rejects any large effort in the Eastern Atlantic area on the grounds that any war on the Central Front will be over before sea power can have any effect. This 'short-war' view had a certain vogue among influential people a few years ago. The objections are simple: if you plan for that length of war, you are planning to lose it, for either you will be overwhelmed or you will have to use nuclear weapons early, and there are no winners in a nuclear war; moreover such a notion forms no part of NATO doctrine; and finally the utility of naval forces for a host of other contingencies is ignored.

These two forms of dissent would emasculate the Navy. A third, conversely, simply wants a much bigger and more powerful Navy on grounds that may unkindly be called sentimental. Its proponents tend to deal in slogans more than reasoned argument, some of the favourites being 'The Lessons of Two World Wars', the 'Protection of Trade', 'Our Island Race', and 'The World Wide Soviet Threat'. All have the seeds of enough truth to be quite good slogans, but when they are not backed by cool rational argument and take no account of political and economic facts they can be counter-productive.

There is, however, a mainstream alternative view. It has been put forward by several influential writers on political and strategic subjects, by research organisations, and by Britain's most prestigious national newspaper, and it cannot be dismissed as sentimental. It can be summarised as follows.

There are two main objections to the official line. First, it subordinates Britain's national interests, which are unique, to NATO strategy and policy. This is most apparent in the termination of the NATO area at the Tropic of Cancer, so that the Southern Atlantic, the Indian and the Pacific Oceans, to say nothing of goings-on in their increasingly unstable, threatened and very important peripheries, do not come within the purview of NATO except by special arrangement. This omission is held not only to be against Britain's interests but against those of oil- and trade-dependent Western Europe as a whole. Nevertheless, it is said (and there is some evidence to support the assertion) the alliance, as an alliance, is extremely reluctant to take any more active interest beyond its present boundary. NATO's influence on British force structures and deployments is also held to be disproportionate, in that it emphasises the Central Front and insists on forward defence, thus locking very substantial British forces into Europe when they could and should be deployed to have more freedom of action.

Secondly, the criterion of 'a contribution to NATO' is singularly vague. It probably started as a phrase invented by civil servants to please ministers. How big is a contribution?

And when the next set of cuts comes along, how can it be argued that what is left does not still constitute a contribution? Staff attempts to give precision to the contribution that Britain ought to make have resulted in the listing of Eastern Atlantic tasks in the way that has already been described, and these have been amalgamated to form a kind of scenario, or determinant case, on which force structures are founded. But it is a vulnerable basis, open to objections that other NATO partners could make a bigger contribution; that the task is not as great or important as the Navy suggests; or that it ought to be done in a different and more economical way. These are the sort of loopholes that are exploited by the Treasury, and it was the third in particular that led to the change of emphasis in 'The Way Forward'; a change which, as is clear from subsequent publications, was made against professional naval advice that the defence in depth necessary for successful anti-submarine warfare would be lost. It is unfortunately also true that forces founded on a single scenario will always be found wanting when the unexpected occurs.

The alternative view therefore rejects a strategy based entirely on current NATO thinking and a single scenario. British strategy ought to be based on the preservation of British vital interests and take account of the uniqueness of our position, both its strengths and vulnerabilities. Such a strategy would accept that British forces were to be provided first and foremost for British national defence needs, and would be justified on those criteria. A large proportion of them would still be assigned to NATO, but their shape and balance would reflect British perceptions of interest and threat, and therefore they would almost certainly be more suitable than now for operations outside the NATO area, and would emphasise mobility, flexibility and adaptability to a variety of tasks.

Of course an immediately favourable reaction from NATO could not be expected. Yet, argue proponents of the alternative view, the alliance might soon understand that such a development was in its long-term interest. And after all, no NATO member other than Britain structures its forces for NATO's benefit with such altruistic abandon. They have national needs for which they provide national forces which are then, in part, assigned to the alliance. Moreover they exact a large price in modifications to NATO strategy, Germany's quite natural insistence on forward defence being the most striking. If Britain adopted a defence structure more suited to its national needs, while at the same time reiterating its commitment to the alliance, no member could properly raise a voice against it. Moreover, NATO cannot stand still. Procedure-bound, slow-moving, set in its ways, worried about money and failing powers, fearful of the future, it shows every sign of advancing middle age. Shock treatment may save it, static senility will certainly kill it.

The details of the maritime forces and concepts of operation that flow from such an alternative strategy have a place in later chapters of this book, particularly the last. It is enough to say here that they should be adaptable, in Sir James Cable's telling phrase, to 'meet a range of risks at sea', and to do so autonomously. That is the whole essence of a national strategy. Because our resources are limited, we should have to set limits to that autonomy; it will be better to leave discussion of those limits until the last chapter.

Nothing in this alternative view detracts from the theory of deterrence, nor from the practice of flexibility in deterrence. Indeed, the ability to conduct operations at various levels of conflict, to reinforce and escalate, backed by suitable diplomatic policy and sensible deployments, is integral to the

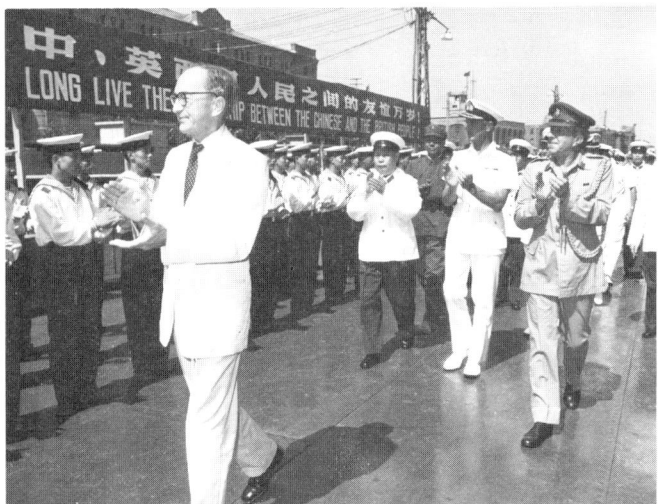

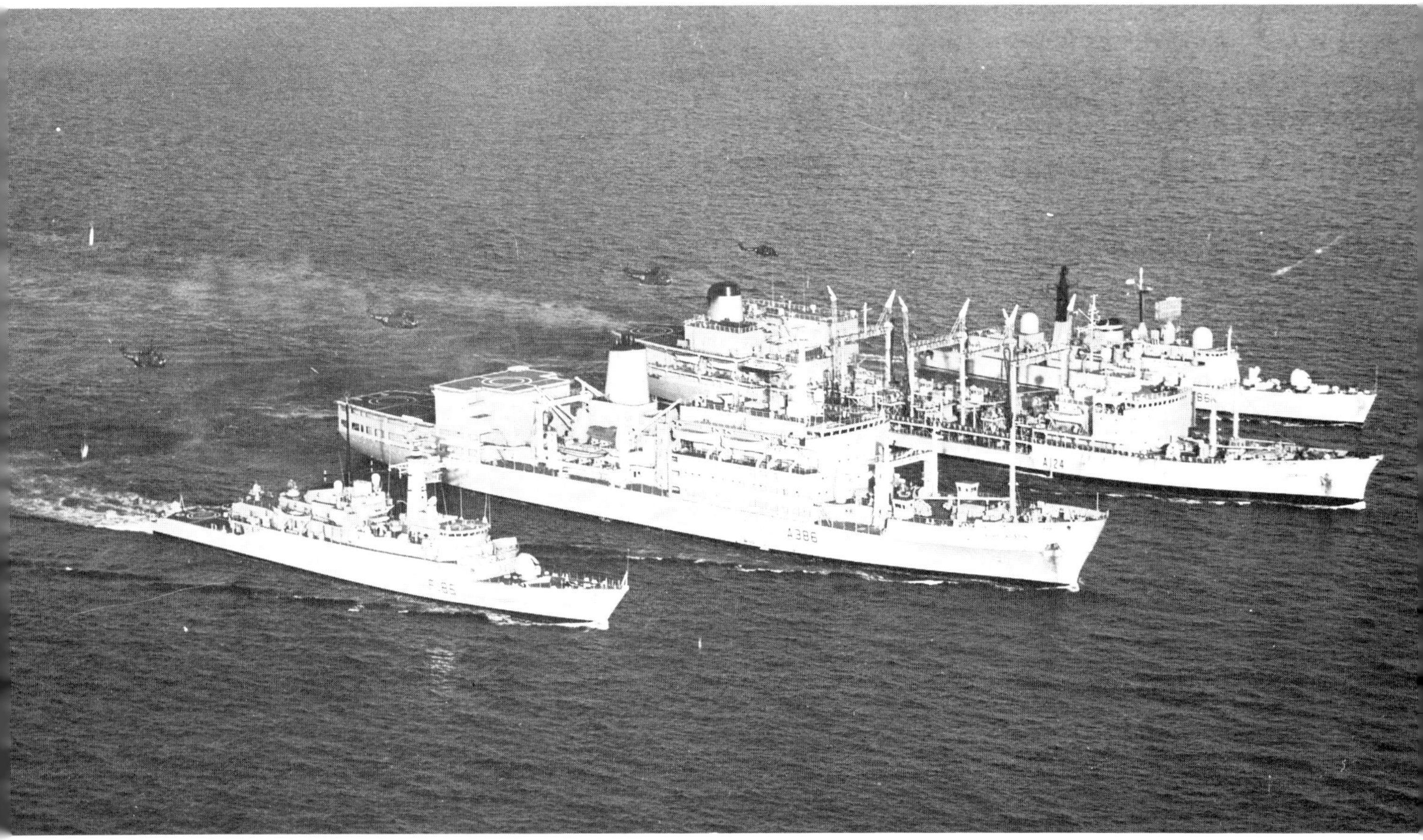

Above:
British wider defence interests must not be neglected. Frigates and support ships on patrol in the Gulf of Oman.
Crown Copyright

Left:
The least assertive aspect of sea power, but still a valuable one: in 1980 the Royal Navy paid its first visit to China for many years.
Crown Copyright

economical execution of a national strategy. So long as that capability is credible, it is not necessary to have expensive maritime garrisons scattered throughout the world.

Even within limits, autonomy does not come cheap; and most proponents of the alternative view accept that, in the absence of an overall increase in defence spending, it would be necessary to make some downward adjustment of the British forces in Germany. The change, it is generally accepted, would be gradual; and there are those who argue that a reduction in British Forces Germany will be essential by the early 1990s anyway on balance-of-payments grounds.

The alternative view was nascent in the late 1970s but its exposure was much increased by the 'Way Forward' document and the South Atlantic campaign. The occurrence, within a few months of each other, of a sharp reduction in government's provision for autonomous surface forces, and then of the demonstrated need for such forces in action, was a natural catalyst for debate. What struck this observer was the clear expectation of the British people that their Navy *would* be capable of independent operations in support of an opposed landing at a distance of 8,000 miles from its main base and against modern medium-power forces. Only the professionals knew how near-run a thing it would be, and how lucky the Navy, and the government, was that the planned reductions, including the sale of HMS *Invincible*, had not yet taken effect. They would, indeed, have set the limits of autonomy too low to give any reasonable prospect of success.

Summary

Those, then, are the two main views of the task for sea power as exercised by British maritime forces: the contribution to NATO and the national strategy. There are, of course, many common elements, and the force structures produced will not vary greatly between the one and the other. But those variations will be significant and could, in the event, be of critical importance. The next eight chapters will discuss the components of our fighting and deterrent power at sea; after that, it will be time to consider an overall assessment.

3 Submarines

There are several good reasons for beginning the more detailed section of this book with a chapter on submarines. First, submarines are with some justification claimed – and not only by submariners – as the most potent of maritime striking forces. Second, the proportion of maritime defence resources that goes into submarine procurement, maintenance and running costs increases year by year; the Royal Navy is already the most submarine-orientated in the Western World, and present plans will move it further in that direction. Finally, submarines operate in, not on or above, the sea; and it is the sea environment that gives sea warfare its unique character.

The Environment

The celebrated truisms about the sea covering 70% of the earth's surface, and about no place on earth being more than 1,720 nautical miles from the sea, are worth repeating. Such a very large body of water is likely to be complex and imperfectly understood, and it is. A tremendous amount of research has gone into the study of the sea, its characteristics and resources. The Russians have over 100 oceanographic ships, the Americans not far short of that number; the Royal Navy, with far fewer, has done much pioneering work in the field. There is still much to learn, particularly in the remoter areas. But many general facts are (as the Russians say) well known.

The sea is largely impenetrable by waves in the electro-magnetic spectrum. This means that both radio (except at very low frequencies indeed) and radar are useless under water. Light finds the sea hard to penetrate, and thermal and wave effects from a submerged body are so far extremely difficult to distinguish from random phenomena.

This leaves sound as the principal means of sensing under water. It travels well through the sea; in the dense water medium the ripple of molecules bumping against each other, which is effectively what sound is, becomes relatively efficient. Porpoises have the right mechanisms built in; humans have had to devise machines, and have progressed pretty quickly, all things considered. The human method of sensing is called sonar: passive sonar is essentially listening by hydrophones for the sounds made by underwater vehicles; active sonar is emitting pulses of sound and listening for echoes from underwater vehicles.

But sound is not conducted through water in a uniform way. This is because temperature, pressure and salinity in the sea vary with depth and climatic conditions and these variations affect the velocity of sound. The consequence is the bending of sound rays as they pass through variations in sea conditions, resulting in areas or bands of very poor or, conversely, unusually good sound reception from any particular source. The situation is further complicated by the presence in the sea of vast numbers of independent noise sources, living and non-living: whales, crustacea, fish, storms and turbulence. When active sonar is employed, reflections from living creatures and from the bottom further confuse the situation.

A submerged vehicle, therefore, that is itself very quiet – thus making it intrinsically difficult for a listening 'passive' observer to hear it – and can in addition position itself at the best depth for concealment (giving the least chance for its own noise, or its echoes to active sonar, to be heard by an observer) is a long way towards escaping aural detection. Since the inception of sonar it has been the ambition of the submarine to achieve this desirable state, preferably throughout a patrol, certainly for as long as possible.

Conventional and Nuclear-Powered Submarines

From about 1900 to 1960 the submarine warship was, with rare exceptions, a somewhat hybrid craft that came a long way from the ideal suggested above, because it was not fully independent of the surface. The only way of propelling it under water was by battery-driven electric motors; the batteries needed recharging at frequent intervals; the only way to recharge the batteries was to run the diesel engines; the diesel

Below:
Launch of a nuclear-powered submarine at Vickers Shipbuilders' yard, Barrow-in-Furness. *Crown Copyright*

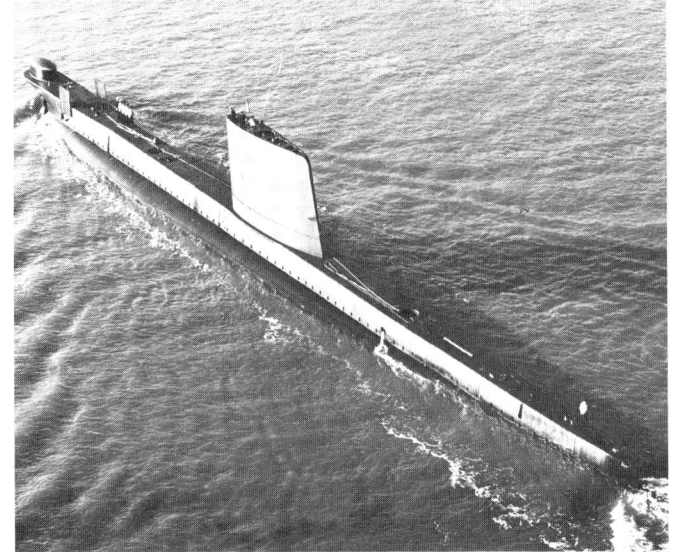

Left:
HMS *Osiris*, a conventionally powered patrol submarine. While this class has given excellent service, providing great advantages in silent and economical operation, most of the boats are over 20 years old and must soon be replaced. *Crown Copyright*

engines needed air to operate. Even the use of the Snort induction mast, though it allowed the submarine to suck in air with its hull beneath the surface, exposed the boat to detection by aircraft radars and put it in an acoustically bad position in the surface sound duct. The snorting mode was noisy, too.

These difficulties were swept away by the application of nuclear propulsion to the submarine. A nuclear reactor working through a heat exchanger to power a steam turbine formed a closed-cycle system independent of the atmosphere; the system did not, moreover, need refuelling in the conventional sense. The problem of stale air within the submarine, which would otherwise have limited underwater endurance, was solved by a combination of devices. An electrolyser produced oxygen through the electrolysis of sea water, carbon dioxide scrubbers maintained CO_2 at acceptable levels, and further filtration processes kept other harmful gases, such as carbon monoxide and freon, well in bounds. Nuclear power brought other great benefits: submarine hull form was improved, speed and manoeuvrability under water were much increased, and the nuclear plant made available ample power to drive sensor, processing and weapon systems as well as domestic services. It is therefore quite correct to call the nuclear-powered boat the first true submarine, and to represent it as a quantum jump in underwater and indeed naval warfare. True, because of the auxiliary machinery that it needs, it can never be as quiet as a diesel-electric submarine on motors, and it is not at ease in shallow water. And when it is being used tactically it has to accept constraints like any other submarine. But there is absolutely no doubt that by embarking

Below:
A much simplified explanation of the effect of sound propagation under water on submarine detection. A submarine 'above the layer' can be detected at relatively long ranges by active sonars or sonobuoys, and noise can be passively detected though interference may reduce range. Below the layer, a submarine is much harder to detect by sensors near the surface, but can still be detected by sensors below the layer. It is also a quieter environment for passive listening. *Bob Downey*

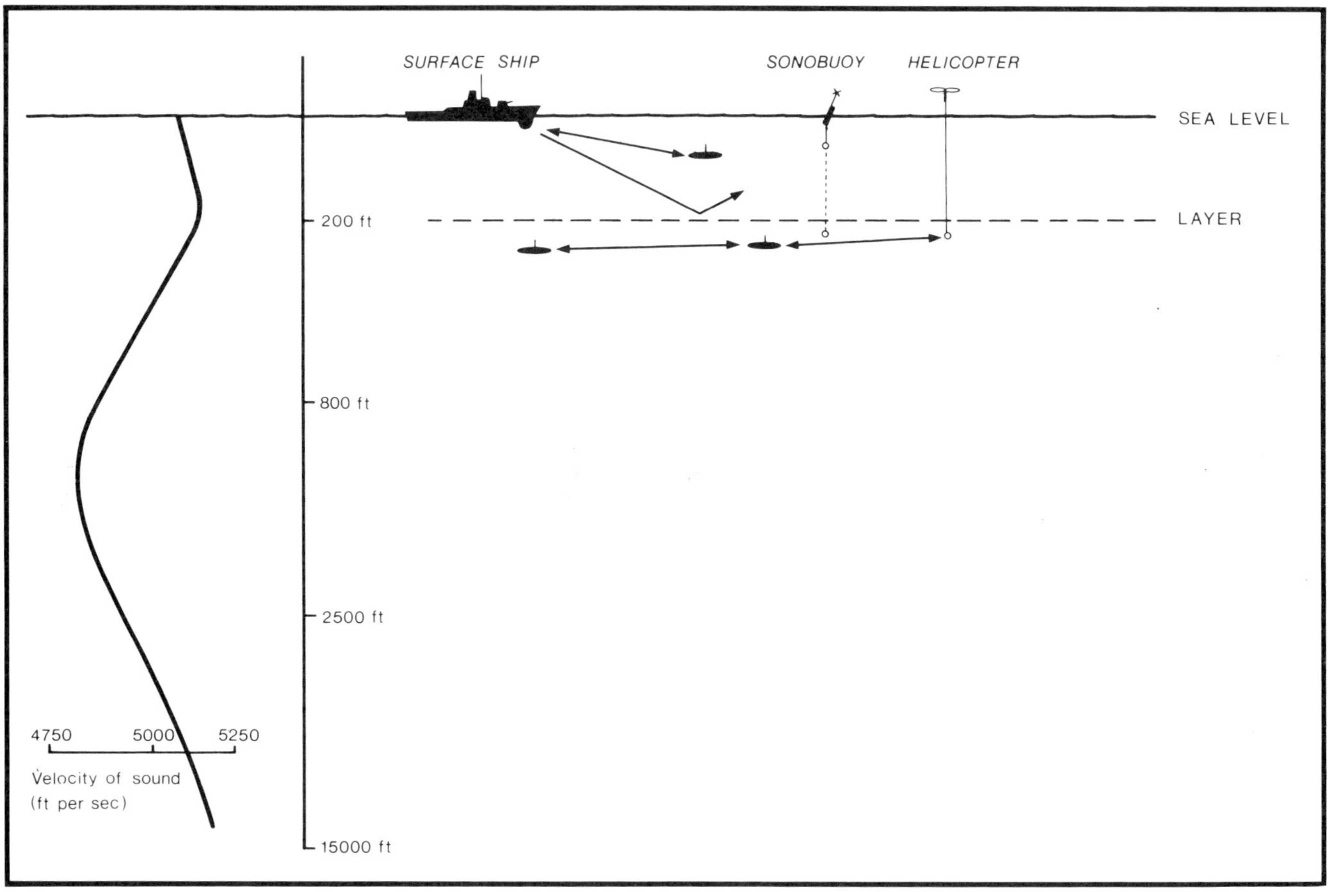
SURFACE SHIP
SONOBUOY
HELICOPTER
SEA LEVEL
LAYER
200 ft
800 ft
2500 ft
15000 ft
4750
5000
5250
Velocity of sound
(ft per sec)

early on a programme of nuclear-powered submarines, the Royal Navy kept itself in the front rank of maritime fighting powers. It is not chance that confines that front rank to the five nations that are also possessors of nuclear weapons and are the permanent members of the United Nations Security Council.

Typical Submarine Operations

Diving and Surfacing

These are the most basic of submarine operations but it is helpful to understand how they are done. The pressure hull of a submarine, in which all the living, machinery, control and weapon spaces are contained, is penetrated in as few places as possible. The ballast tanks which regulate the buoyancy may be external to the pressure hull or contained within it, but in any event must have valves which give access to the sea. When the submarine dives, these valves are opened to admit water to the ballast tanks; positive buoyancy is destroyed and the submarine sinks, aided by the action of hydroplanes which act like the elevators of an aircraft. At the desired depth neutral buoyancy in achieved by adjustment of the water remaining in trimming tanks within the pressure hull, and minor manoeuvres in the vertical plane are carried out by means of the hydroplanes. When the submarine wishes to surface, compressed air is blown into the ballast tanks from sources within the pressure hull, positive buoyancy is restored and – usually aided by the hydroplanes – the submarine rises to the surface.

Attacks on Surface Units

Submarines at depth can often hear surface units a great way off with their passive hydrophone equipments including, these days, arrays towed behind the more sophisticated submarines. The characteristic frequency patterns of such detections may give a good indication of the type – sometimes even the identity – of the target, and its bearing. But they will not measure range; only active sonar, with its fixed time-base given by the emission of the 'ping', and its measurement of the time taken for the echo to return, can do that, and submarines

do not like to use it because it announces their presence. So ranges from passive sonar must be estimates, constantly refined with computer assistance but never certain.

A submarine which decides to attack with a stand-off missile will clearly want to be reasonably sure that the target range is within the missile envelope, and also to have an idea of the target's course and speed so that the missile may be sent off on the right course to intercept. This again cannot be more than an estimate. For very long range missiles, mid-course guidance may be necessary, and this entails the submarine's breaking surface to expose its guidance radar. Some Russian submarines work this way; Western ones, using shorter-range missiles, do not. Whatever is done in mid-course, submarine-launched missiles normally have autonomous, active radar terminal homing which is switched on when approaching the target area. Like any other automatic system, the homing head's ability to identify is not infallible and it may be subject to spoofing.

There are, then considerations which may make a submarine prefer to close and attack with torpedoes; and some are armed only with torpedoes anyway. Torpedo attack generally entails manoeuvring in to quite close ranges, of the order of a few thousand yards. This usually means the use by the submarine of speeds faster than prudence would dictate. It may, if it stays deep, have to use active sonar to achieve a fire control solution; conversely, if it comes shallow to use its periscope, it will be in the surface duct. If it uses a wire-guided torpedo its manoeuvres are constrained while the torpedo is running; but unguided torpedoes, which allow it to evade after firing, are less certain of hitting a manoeuvring target. Torpedo attack, therefore, is very likely to expose the submarine to detection. Whether it is in fact detected depends on how numerous, well-positioned and alert the anti-submarine forces are; and on how well the submarine is handled; and on luck.

Attacks on Enemy Submarines

The advent of nuclear-powered submarines, advances in passive sonar, increased knowledge of the part played by sea water conditions in acoustic detection and the invention of self-homing torpedoes have all helped to make it possible to

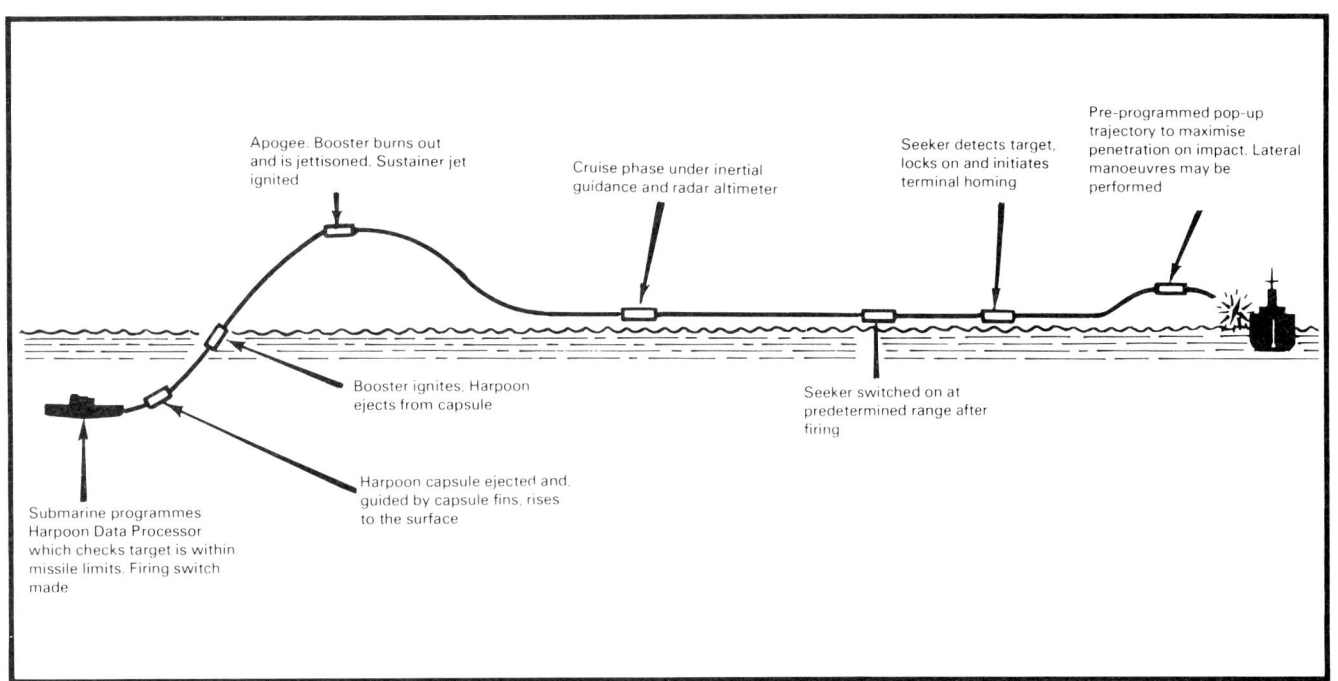

Apogee. Booster burns out and is jettisoned. Sustainer jet ignited

Cruise phase under inertial guidance and radar altimeter

Seeker detects target, locks on and initiates terminal homing

Pre-programmed pop-up trajectory to maximise penetration on impact. Lateral manoeuvres may be performed

Booster ignites, Harpoon ejects from capsule

Seeker switched on at predetermined range after firing

Harpoon capsule ejected and, guided by capsule fins, rises to the surface

Submarine programmes Harpoon Data Processor which checks target is within missile limits. Firing switch made

Above left:
Conventional submarines are much more suitable than nuclear-powered boats for operations close inshore.
Crown Copyright

Above:
Harpoon operational sequence. *Author*

conceive of the submarine as an anti-submarine system, and all advanced navies now put this role high on their lists of priorities.

Initial detection of an opposing submarine may be greatly aided by pre-warning from other sources, such as the passive sonar arrays laid in certain parts of the ocean and monitored from shore, or patrolling aircraft. But whether alerted or not, an anti-submarine submarine will expect to make its first detection by passive sonar. In doing this it will be greatly helped if its design gives it 'sonar advantage', that is to say if its own noise is less strong, and its sonars more sensitive, than those of the opposition. It will also be helped if there are no extraneous noises; sorting out the characteristic submarine sounds in a busy environment may be a laborious process.

The later stages of an attack are a study in quiet (indeed ultra-quiet: try dropping a teacup and see how popular you are) drama. The boat is manoeuvred to remain at the optimum depth, and the computer is fed with the enemy's bearing, own course and speed and any range indications there may be. Various solutions for enemy course, speed and range are 'tried' on the computer, which indicates those that are most compatible with the known data. Eventually the attacking Commanding Officer judges that he is in a position to fire and releases as many torpedoes as are judged necessary. These, often wire-guided from the submarine, have acoustic heads which are designed to home on the target once they are within a certain range. Another way of attacking target submarines, from longer range, is by air-flight missile with either a nuclear depth charge or acoustic torpedo as its terminal device.

Operations with the Fleet and Independent Patrols
But submarines, even in wartime, are not constantly employed

in making attacks. There are two basic modes of operation at other times. Operating with a surface force tends to mean that a submarine, normally a nuclear-powered boat, is allocated a station or area which moves as the force moves. In order to avoid what is politely called mutual interference (and impolitely called getting clobbered by one's own side) good navigation and routine – though not constant – communication are called for. This is not easy, particularly as communication through the water is still chancy and radio communication may entail operating at anything but optimum depth; but with its good sonar sensors a submarine can be a great asset to a surface force.

When all is said and done, though, most submarines prefer an independent life away from the immediate vicinity of friendly surface units, stalking their prey whether submarine or surface ship, untrammelled by any doubt as to its enemy character. They are of course well suited to excursions into waters infested by hostile forces. Their ability to make such penetrations gives them an important peacetime surveillance capability.

Strategic Deterrent Patrols
A form of submarine operation that has come into being in the past 20 years is the deterrent patrol with strategic nuclear missiles. The object is to maintain at immediate readiness the ability to inflict unacceptable damage on the opponent. The submarine must therefore be kept at sea, undetected, within range of its targets in the homeland of a potential enemy. This entails quiet, discreet operation and above all the avoidance of trouble. Such tactical weapons as strategic deterrent submarines possess are for self-defence, to be used only as a last resort if by any chance the submarine is detected and comes under attack in wartime.

British Submarines

Patrol Submarines
Unlike the United States Navy, which has virtually ceased to operate diesel-electric submarines, the Royal Navy still has a number of these 'conventional' boats – 15 at present, which is

23

almost the same number as the nuclears. They were built in the early 1960s but are not just left-overs being run down; not only are they regarded as having a specific role, but plans for their replacement by a new class, the Type 2400, are in an advanced stage and the first order, for HMS *Upholder*, was placed in 1983.

The rationale for the continued use of patrol submarines is threefold. First, they are intrinsically quieter than nuclear boats. Therefore, in certain areas where the opponent's freedom of manoeuvre may be constrained, they can lurk undetected with a good chance of getting into action. Second, they are much cheaper than nuclear boats and so overall numbers can be higher than with an all-nuclear fleet. Third, they are very useful in the training role – both to break in submariners from Able Seamen to newly-qualified Commanding Officers who have, after, some years in submarines of all sorts, passed their 'Perisher' course; and to act as targets for anti-submarine units.

Present patrol submarines are mainly of the 'Oberon' class. Propulsion on the surface is by Admiralty designed V-16 mechanically supercharged diesel engines, and when submerged by two electric motors supplied – as is power throughout the boat – by two batteries each of 224 cells (440V DC) made by Chloride Ltd. Submerged speed is up to 17kt, but at very high speeds the batteries become exhausted in a matter of hours. Use of low speeds can stretch this to some days.

The main weapon is the torpedo; the 'O' class has six bow and two stern tubes with stowage for 20 and four torpedoes respectively. The wire-guided acoustic homing torpedo Tigerfish is carried mainly for anti-submarine work; it can be used also for attacking surface ships, as can the old but reliable Mk 8** which is still in service.

It is fair to say that shortage of power and space has a critical effect on every aspect of life in a patrol submarine. Conditions are cramped, facilities for washing are limited, and food tends to become monotonous after a few days at sea. With a crew of seven officers and 62 ratings, a patrol submarine needs a very high degree of dedication and knowledge from every crew member. This breeds mutual trust that is at once apparent in the relaxed, informal yet totally disciplined atmosphere that exists throughout the boat.

Even the Type 2400 will remain in essence the kind of boat just described. Certainly there will be many improvements. High generator output and battery capacity will decrease the required snorting time and increase the amount of power

Right:
HMS *Dreadnought*, the first nuclear-powered submarine in the Royal Navy.
Crown Copyright, photograph by Leading Airman Eric Rooke

Below:
The nuclear-powered fleet submarine *Conqueror* leaving Faslane. The pear-shaped hull form is rather cumbersome on the surface but highly efficient when dived. *Crown Copyright*

The weapons fitted have tended to lag behind the boats' excellent intrinsic qualities, but in the last few years a great advance has been made in anti-ship capability with the acquisition of the Harpoon missile. This American weapon is fired from a 21in torpedo tube, is 15½ft long and weighs some 1,500lb. On firing (by compressed air, as are torpedoes) it ascends to the surface, its rocket motor ignites, its stub wings unfold, and it sets off on a preset course towards its target, the homing head being activated as it approaches the target area. The warhead is high explosive. The flight path is at low altitude, making the missile difficult to detect by radar. Maximum range is approximately 60 miles, but the actual firing range will of course be dependent on a satisfactory fire control solution.

Torpedoes in fleet submarines are the same as in patrol submarines. A Tigerfish successor, the Spearfish, which uses much improved homing logic that should effectively counter attempted spoofing measures, is expected to come into service before 1990.

Life in a fleet submarine has more of the trappings of civilisation to it than patrol submarine existence. Although the boat is submerged nearly all the time when at sea, air is kept fresh and hot water and cooking facilities are abundant. All this is due to the ample power supplies provided by the nuclear plant. Moreover, there is more space so that every man has his own bunk and lockers are quite roomy by submarine standards. But the need for teamwork, and the response to that need by the crew, are still crucial, and there is no lack of verve in the handling of these boats. They are always very conscious of their own potential, but this was given extra impetus by the knowledge that, after the sinking of the *General Belgrano* by

available, and a smaller complement (44 in all) will be able to make better use of the carefully designed domestic arrangements; weapon control will be more precise and the variety of weapons available will be enhanced by air-flight missiles. But the difference is in degree, not kind. That is provided only by the nuclear-powered submarine.

Fleet Submarines
In 1984 the Royal Navy had some 13 nuclear-powered fleet submarines in service and the force is planned to build up to a steady figure of 17 by the late 1980s. The first such boat, HMS *Dreadnought*, was a one-off design with an American powerplant. The rest, from *Valiant* onwards, have all-British machinery and have followed a steady evolutionary pattern. Improvements made to successive boats have included quietening measures, better passive sonar performance and data processing – including, it is clear, towed arrays in some vessels – and more advanced main and auxiliary machinery.

HMS *Conqueror* (with Mk 8** torpedoes, incidentally), the Argentine Navy was kept in harbour by the threat of the fleet submarines.

Ballistic Missile Submarines
The British Polaris project, begun in 1962, was a startling example of swift and ordered technical development and production. In just under seven years, four very large nuclear-powered submarines were designed and built, equipped with American-made missiles with British warheads, and completed so that since 1969 there has never been a moment when the British Polaris force did not have at least one submarine on patrol.

The Polaris submarines share many characteristics with the fleet boats; their powerplants, ancillary systems and many of their sensors are common. The armament is, however, quite different. The whole midship section is taken up with 16 vertical tubes each housing a Polaris missile. These are 31ft long, solid fuelled, two-stage ballistic missiles. Each carries, in addition to its nuclear warheads, the new Chevaline modification which is designed to counter improved Soviet antiballistic missile measures by a combination of hardening against nuclear counter-attack and presenting the defences with

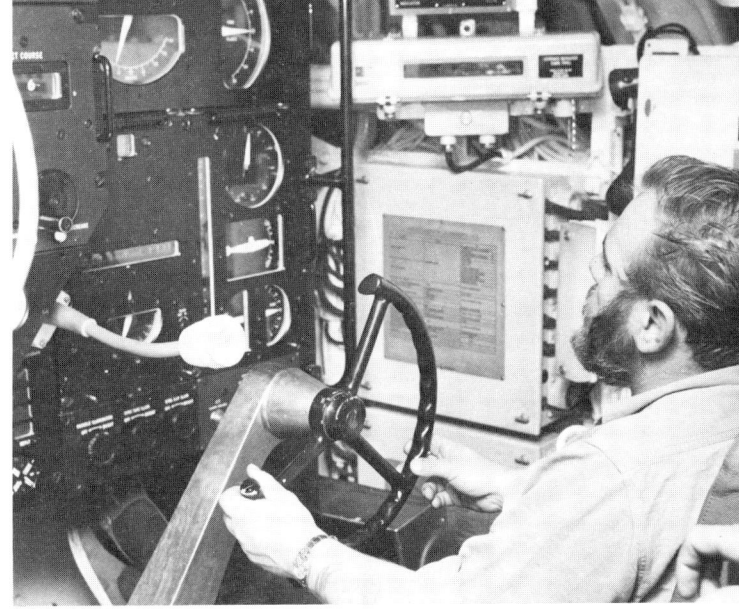

Above right:
On board the fleet submarine *Warspite*, the foreplanesman controls the attitude of the submarine in the vertical plane. *Crown Copyright*

Right:
The nuclear-powered fleet submarine *Sovereign* at the North Pole, October 1976. After 10 days under the icecap, conducting geophysical survey work, the submarine surfaced through a polynya – a patch of relatively thin ice. *Crown Copyright*

Below:
Spearfish, the Royal Navy's new heavyweight anti-submarine torpedo. *Marconi Underwater Systems*

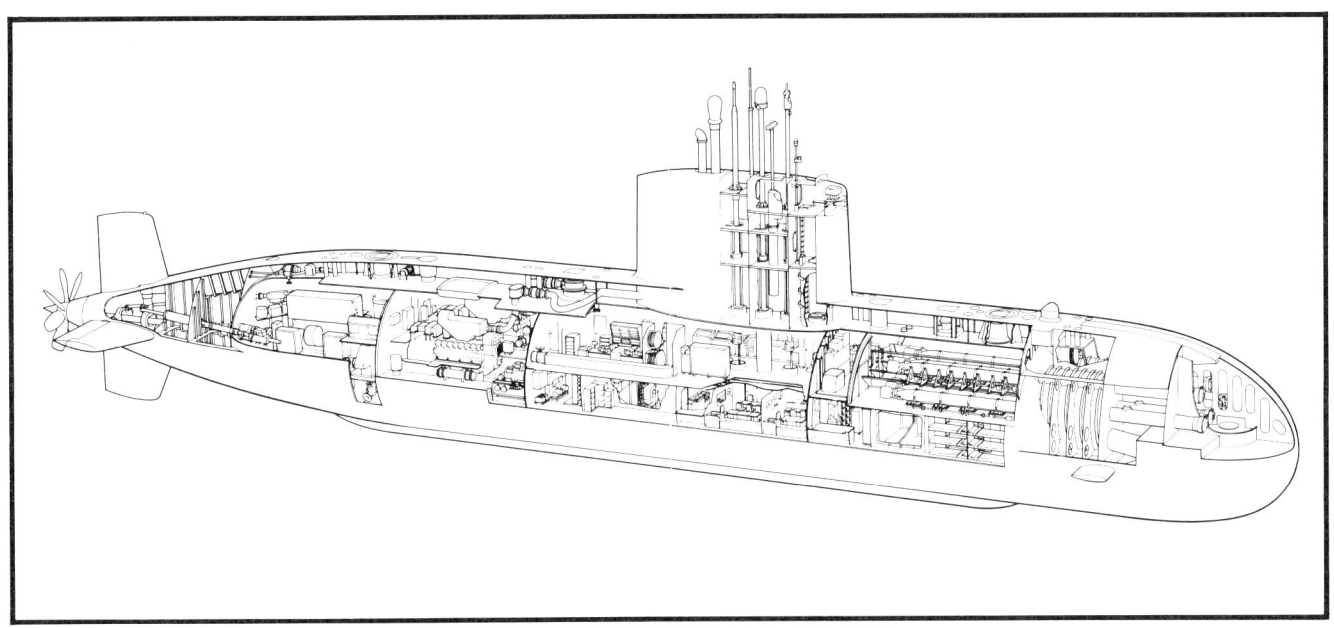

a large number of widely-separated decoy targets in space.

Control of the system, which gives to each submarine a firepower greater than all the bombs dropped by both sides in World War 2, is in the hands of the British Government. The primary means of transmitting an order to fire would be by very low frequency radio; back-up means of transmission exist but are a closely guarded secret. Once a firing message is received on board, it must be independently authenticated to the Captain by two officers using entirely different authentication data. The boat's position is kept precisely up to date by the Ship Inertial Navigation System (SINS – another system shared with fleet submarines) and this is fed to the missile launch computers along with the target co-ordinates. Guidance requirements are worked out and cross-checked. Missile launch is by high-pressure gas, and guidance, once the missile is clear of the water and ignited, by an inertial system within the missile. At a predetermined moment the guidance system switches off the rocket motors, and the re-entry bodies separate from the rest of the missile, following a ballistic trajectory to the target.

The ability to go through that sequence, at any moment during a patrol of 60 days or so, is the Polaris submarine's whole reason for being. It is its business to remain undetected, and it has been stated by ministers that there is good reason to believe that the Soviet Union has never found one of our submarines on patrol.

All the amenities of a fleet submarine are available also in the Polaris boat. The food is, indeed, even better, and the films tend to be more modern. Static recreation – rowing machines and get-nowhere bicycles – is provided. Each crew member can receive news from home once a week, by what is called a familygram; much ingenuity goes into fitting into 40 words all that need be said, particularly as there is no possibility of replies from the boat, which of course keeps strict radio silence throughout its patrol.

To get maximum utilisation from Polaris submarines, each has two crews of 13 officers and 130 ratings who man her for alternate patrols; the off-duty crew are ashore at the Faslane base undergoing refresher training, taking leave, breaking in new crew members, spending some time with their families and preparing to go back to sea. The Polaris submarines have a certain gravitas; this is partly because of the high standard of

Above:
Line drawing of the Royal Navy's new class of patrol submarine, the Type 2400. *Vickers Shipbuilders*

Below:
The integrated monitoring panel in the missile compartment of the Polaris submarine *Resolution*. *Crown Copyright*

British Submarines

Name and Pendant No		Completed	Length feet (metres)	Beam feet (metres)	Speed Submerged knots	Complement
Ballistic Missile Submarines						
Resolution	(S22)					
Renown	(S26)	1967-69	425	33	25	Two crews
Repulse	(S23)		(129.5)	(10.1)		of 147
Revenge	(S27)					
Fleet Submarines						
Valiant	(S102)	1966-67	285	33	28	116
Warspite	(S103)		(86.8)	(10.1)		
Churchill	(S104)		285	33	28	116
Conqueror	(S105)	1968-73	(86.8)	(10.1)		
Courageous	(S106)					
Swiftsure	(S126)					
Sovereign	(S108)					
Superb	(S109)	1973-81	272	33	30+	116
Sceptre	(S110)		(82.9)	(10.1)		
Spartan	(S111)					
Splendid	(S112)					
Trafalgar	(S113)					
Turbulent	(S114)					
Tireless	(S115)	1983-	Not released			130
Torbay	(S116)					
Trenchant	(S91)					
one ordered						
Patrol Submarines						
Sealion	(S07)	1958-61	295	26	17	65
Walrus	(S08)		(90)	(7.9)		
Oberon	(S09)					
Odin	(S10)					
Orpheus	(S11)					
Olympus	(S12)					
Osiris	(S13)					
Onslaught	(S14)					
Otter	(S15)	1960-67	295	26	17	65
Oracle	(S16)		(90)	(7.9)		
Ocelot	(S17)					
Otus	(S18)					
Opossum	(S19)					
Opportune	(S20)					
Onyx	(S21)					
Type 2400		Ordered	231	25	20	44
Upholder		1983	(70.3)	(7.6)		

training and therefore the proportion of senior to junior rates, and partly because of the mission itself. It is the least frivolous of all the Navy's jobs.

It is planned to replace the Polaris submarines during the 1990s with a force of four new submarines equipped with Trident D-5 missiles. Each submarine will carry 16 missiles, which given the multiple-warhead capability of the D-5 will be of greater penetration and destructive power than is strictly necessary for British deterrent requirements. It is clear from published government documents from 1980 onwards that this point has been studied extensively, as has every other aspect of the Polaris replacement. The Trident submarines will incorporate a new reactor, the PWR2, with a longer core life, and the most advanced sonars.

Conclusion

Submarines are a vastly important part of any modern navy: nuclear-powered submarines confer a great increment of maritime power, ballistic missile submarines one of fundamental state power. Yet it is important to remember that submarines have their limitations and that there are some things they cannot do. Patrol and fleet submarines can seek to deny the use of the sea to opponents; they cannot fully safeguard its use by one's own side, they cannot conduct air defence, they cannot carry substantial cargoes or large numbers of troops. If they attempt to control the surface, in peace, tension or war, they act out of character and temporarily lose all their advantages. As for ballistic missile submarines, they use the sea for but one purpose: strategic deterrence. It is too soon in this book to attempt an overall appraisal and balance, but not too soon perhaps to knock one particular phrase on the head. 'The submarine is the Capital Ship of the future' will not stand up even to this cursory analysis. The realities of modern conflict at sea are too complex to permit such a simple slogan.

Left:
A British Polaris missile on a test firing. *Crown Copyright*

Below:
In the health physics laboratory of HMS *Resolution*.
Crown Copyright

4 The Surface Fleet

Most uses of the sea involve an ability to occupy a part of its surface. Transport (both for peaceable and warlike purposes), the exploration and exploitation of resources, research and recreation, all overwhelmingly demand the use of the interface between water and air. It is not surprising, for man is a creature of the interface himself.

It does not automatically follow that surface warships are necessary. Submarines and shore-based aircraft, if they were of sufficient numbers, power and flexibility, if they knew well enough what was going on, and if their actions could be well co-ordinated, might deploy enough strength totally to deny the sea to opposing forces of all sorts, so that surface uses by their own side could continue.

This is not a likely situation, either on the face of it or on deeper analysis. To be effective, the denial would have to be virtually complete; once opposing forces could muster in any strength they would wreak havoc against the surface users. The philosophy would demand, in fact, a command of the sea more absolute than Mahan, in his simple two-dimensional world, ever dreamed of.

Thus, even if cost and effectiveness considerations are discounted, there is still an apparent need for some surface warships. In fact, as this and later chapters will show, there are many functions that such vessels can carry out more economically than any other maritime vehicle. The trick, of course, is to get the balance right, not only as between surface vessels and other maritime forces, but within the surface fleet itself. This last problem is not helped by the bewildering number of options that now present themselves in the above-water environment.

The Above-Water Environment

While almost as complex as the sea beneath it, the earth's atmosphere is less baffling as an environment in which to fight. The chief aberrations are caused by weather conditions and are generally of less severe and lasting effect than those under the surface, provided that technology and expertise exist to overcome them.

Electromagnetic waves travel well in the atmosphere. Because they go at the speed of light and because variations in them are very quickly and precisely detectable by modern electronics, extremely large quantities of data can be transmitted, received and exchanged. The main limitation is that most electromagnetic waves will in normal conditions follow only a straight line path. There is an exception in the high-frequency band, where waves bounce off the ionosphere and so skip round the world, but so far as ships are concerned it is useful only for communication.

As in the subsurface environment, sensors can be active or passive. Radar, the chief active sensor, operates basically by emitting very short pulses of radio energy at frequencies of 200kHz upwards, and receiving and processing the energy reflected by air or surface targets. Bearing is given by the direction in which the aerial is pointing, range by measuring electronically the time the pulse takes to go out and return. Radar performance can be degraded by sea, cloud and rain returns, but modern techniques can minimise these – at a price. Radar can also be jammed by emitters working on its frequency, but nowadays it is possible to shift that frequency very rapidly.

The majority of passive sensors are designed to detect, and find the direction of, opposing radar and radio transmissions. The laws of physics ensure that an active radar emission can nearly always be detected before it gets an echo from the unit that is passively listening for it – provided, of course, that that unit has suitable equipment and is well trained in its use. But, like nearly all passive systems, it will not generate a range. There are other sensors that do not entail transmitting in the above-water environment; using infra-red and low light television techniques, they are mostly of relatively short range.

Miniaturisation of components has meant that electronic emitters and receivers can now be contained in very small packages, and this has led to their incorporation in air-breathing tactical missiles. Micro-circuitry has allowed programming of missiles to the extent that after launch they can be autonomous. Active or passive radar, infra-red or television homing techniques can all be used, very low altitudes can be achieved by the use of radar altimeters and evasive manoeuvres can be built in.

In all surface-ship operations, the best use and exploitation of the above-water environment is a critical factor.

Typical Surface Ship Operations

Being There
The most common condition of international relations is one of uneasy peace. There are conflicts between nations ranging from differences of view to quite acute disputes; in general these are contained within the bounds of international politics and diplomacy. But, particularly when they concern sea affairs, they often admit the use of naval forces as an expression of concern and involvement.

The fact that a war vessel or maritime aircraft is under government control, is manned by disciplined personnel and can deploy military power means that any opponent confronting it is faced with a difficult choice if he wishes to assail the interests of its owner. He must neutralise it first; but if he seeks to do so, he is likely to be the aggressor and so culpable in international law, and of course he will invite escalation. He might even lose the first round.

Military vessels are thus very good vehicles for demonstrating right and resolve in those areas – and they are

Right:
Still needed for control of the surface: HMS *Brazen*, typical of the modern generation of medium-sized surface ships.
Crown Copyright

30

Above:
Ambuscade, Opportune and Sea King. Co-ordination of air and sub-surface assets is easy enough here, on Staff College Sea Days, but in operational conditions it requires extensive facilities in surface units. *Crown Copyright*

Below:
Port visits: acceptable, low-key military diplomacy.
Crown Copyright

still, in the current or any likely state of the international law of the sea, the vast majority of the sea areas of the world – where they have a right to be. And surface ships are overwhelmingly the best kind of vessel for such a task.

The reasons for this are fairly obvious. Surface ships are eminently controllable, given modern communications. They are visible and overt, making the maximum demonstrative impact. There is little sinister about their image. They can deploy a variety of weapon systems, ranging from the ceremonial to the lethal, giving them many options for the discriminating exercise of force. They can keep the sea for long periods, particularly if they have the necessary support ships. And they can carry aircraft, particularly helicopters, which extend their surveillance and weapon abilities.

Neither submarines nor fixed-wing aircraft have similar advantages in this role. They pack a more lethal punch and are less vulnerable, but their relatively crude application of force is much less suitable to situations where the correct level of violence is often all-important. They suffer from less certain communication and control; and aircraft have endurance problems. Units of this sort are needed to threaten escalation, are fine sticks to shake; but they are not in the game of being there as the surface ship habitually is. One further place where a surface vessel can be is, of course, a foreign port. Ship visits serve a useful diplomatic function in the broadest sense; as parcels of national sovereignty, handsome and swift and manned by sailors with similar characteristics, they can do much to make and cement friendships, to reassure and buttress alliances.

Regulation
If demonstrations of right and resolve in distant waters are part of the surface warship's task, so is the regulation of the coastal and offshore waters of its own state. Some nations employ specially constructed and organised ships in such waters to patrol and enforce state law concerning fisheries, continental shelf resource exploitation, customs, fiscal and immigration matters and pollution control. But whatever these vessels are called, they are still armed and their crews are under disciplined control. Typically, all vessels concerned in these tasks are relatively small, lightly armed, weatherly, well equipped with communications and able to co-operate with the aircraft that are the other essential component of an offshore regulation organisation.

Anti-Surface Vessel Warfare
But the core of a surface warship's being is its ability to fight. Fighting against other surface vessels was for several hundred years almost the only combatant function of warships. Now it is less prominent but is still an essential task.

Jacky Fisher had a dictum: Hit first, hit hard and keep on hitting. It is singularly applicable to modern anti-surface vessel warfare. Hitting first means not only having weapons that outrange the opponent, but which are controllable to be

effective at such long ranges. This implies the ability to acquire the target with the available sensors and to achieve a satisfactory fire control solution, either with ship's equipment or the equipment contained in the weapon itself, so that a hit can be obtained. Hitting hard means that the weapons must have warheads of enough power to cause incapacitating, if not total, destruction. Keeping on hitting has two components: the platform must remain afloat and operational, and enough ammunition must be carried to sustain the fight.

Anti-Submarine Warfare

Surface ships can themselves act as anti-submarine units. They are able to mount powerful active sonars and to tow sensitive passive sonars; the former are likely to give accurate information out to some tens of thousands of yards in good water conditions, the latter to give indications particularly on noisy submarines to much greater distances. Moderate speeds are necessary to achieve results. Weapons systems to match the ranges and accuracies involved are required. Surface ships can also deploy airborne anti-submarine units: some of these – typically large helicopters and small fixed-wing aircraft – will be self-contained search and attack systems, limited mainly by their endurance. Others, typically the smaller helicopters, are deployable mainly to carry weapons to the position of submarines detected by the parent ship or a co-operating unit.

Air Defence

The air threat to surface vessels both armed and unarmed, as was shown by the Falklands conflict, is now endemic in sea fighting. It can take the form of manned aircraft closely pressing home attacks, but more typically in modern warfare is likely to involve air-flight missiles with autonomous terminal homing. Against such threats surface ships of sufficient size and suitable shape may deploy organic fighter aircraft, and a much wider range of surface craft can mount self-contained air defences. These fall into two categories: area defence weapons, which can engage crossing targets and therefore may

Above:
Regulation of coastal waters: HMS _Jersey_ on patrol.
Crown Copyright

Below:
HMS _Nottingham_. This Type 42 destroyer is built primarily for the air defence role, with Sea Dart as its main armament.
Crown Copyright

be used to protect adjacent ships as well as one's own, and point defence weapons which engage approaching targets and defend their parent unit. Surface ships may also deploy measures such as decoys and jammers to minimise the chances of incoming air threats acquiring them as targets.

Command and Control

With its large size, its comprehensive power sources and its position straddling the interface, the surface ship is singularly well placed to exercise command and control over a wide variety of forces above, on and under the sea, and ashore too at an early stage of amphibious operations. This is by no means a subsidiary role. British superiority in command and control was said by an official Argentine report to be one of the principal factors in our success in the South Atlantic campaign. It was indeed then, as so often it had been shown to be in

exercises, a 'force multiplier' that enabled the most effective force to be brought to bear at the right place.

Amphibious Operations

Only surface ships are able to carry large numbers of troops and their equipment to land operationally at a long distance from their base. Airborne forces can, of course, make a lodgment in certain conditions, but sustaining even such an expedition requires seaborne support. The Falklands was an extreme, but not a special, case. Surface ships can support amphibious operations also by bombardment of enemy positions ashore; either guns or shipborne aircraft can be used for such a task.

Balanced Fleet, Rolling Programme

A surface ship that could superlatively well carry out all the fighting functions just listed would be a very large, very expensive vessel. Few indeed, if any, could be afforded by a

Top:
HMS *Intrepid*, a specialised amphibious ship, seen here intercepting the Soviet helicopter cruiser *Moskva* off the North African coast. *Crown Copyright*

Above:
HMS *Invincible*, with post-Falklands armament additions, and upper deck manned, entering harbour. *Crown Copyright*

power with Britain's resource limitations. Even if questions of vulnerability could be set aside, a very small number of such ships would mean only limited cover of all too many commitments. And a very high-capability fighting ship is not appropriate for many tasks that demand a light diplomatic touch.

In consequence the shape of the surface fleet has evolved differently. It consists of a relatively large number of medium-sized vessels, frigates and destroyers, with the ability to carry out all the combatant tasks but to an extent more or less limited by their design and cost; and a very few ships of higher quality, with a considerably greater scope and reach. Typically, the higher quality ships back up the lower, and when the back-up is called in the other arms, submarines and fixed-wing aircraft, can be expected to be deployed also. This is, in short, the concept of a balanced fleet geared to a rational pattern of deterrence and escalation.

The fleet has evolved, as the concept has; neither was new-minted at any stage. This is a normal characteristic of navies, with long-wearing hardware and durable traditions, but it has been particularly marked in the Royal Navy because of its long history, sense of continuity and a material infrastructure that included a shipbuilding industry well-adapted to a steady programme and singularly ill-suited to a spasmodic one. In spite of numerous reappraisals and reversals of decision by successive governments, the development of the surface fleet, viewed in retrospect, has been fairly self-consistent – up to now. The results of this rolling programme, as they stand in the mid-1980s, will now be described.

Aircraft Carriers

The fleet carriers, of which *Eagle* and the previous *Ark Royal* were the last in the Royal Navy, were surface ships of comprehensive power. When it was decided that no comparable successors should be built, some of their tasks – notably the long-range air warning and defence of the fleet – fell to the Royal Air Force. Nevertheless there was still a need to deploy, in numbers, the highly capable anti-submarine helicopters, to provide area air defence and to exercise command of complex and diverse maritime forces. On analysis it emerged that the most cost-effective way of doing these things was to co-locate them in a vessel of 15-20,000 tons displacement, and thus the 'Invincible' class, originally called 'through-deck' cruisers, was conceived. The design's chief external feature was a flat top; this and an all-gas turbine powerplant were firm components of the design from an early stage, as was a Sea Dart area air defence system. The most important later addition was the incorporation of arrangements to operate vertical/short take-off and landing (V/STOL) fixed-wing aircraft. These were thought of initially as giving the ship the ability to deny the airspace round it to enemy reconnaissance, to probe over the horizon for threats, and to threaten strikes against opposing surface units – all at short notice and independently of shore resources. As matters turned out in the South Atlantic campaign, the Sea Harrier was used primarily for fighter air defence and for ground attack against shore targets: an example of the way an innately sound weapon system shows its adaptability.

HMS *Invincible* was built at Barrow-in-Furness by Vickers Shipbuilders Ltd and launched by Her Majesty the Queen in 1977. Her sister ships *Illustrious* and *Ark Royal* were built by Swan Hunters at Wallsend-on-Tyne.

The ship is powered by four Rolls-Royce Olympus TM36 gas turbines rated at 20,850kW each. These drive two David Brown triple-reduction reversing gearboxes and thence to two fixed-pitch propellers. Elaborate cross-feeding arrangements ensure maximum flexibility in case of damage. Electrical power is supplied by eight Paxman Valenta 1,175kW generators; these are in no less than six different machinery spaces so, again, there is much allowance for action damage. Fresh water is supplied by five Stone Platt auxiliary boilers.

Top:
The launch of HMS *Ark Royal*, third of the 'Invincible' class.
Crown Copyright

Above:
In the hangar, HMS *Invincible*. *Crown Copyright*

The whole machinery plant is monitored by the Decca ISIS system in the machinery control room.

The ship's command, control and information system is designed to make the maximum use of all the information sources available, both internal and external. The operations room system includes Ferranti FM1600 computers and Plessey displays for information and fire control. Communications are provided by the proven Marconi ICS3 system, which combined with satellite terminals gives very high flexibility and data rates. Communications was one of the greatest success stories of the South Atlantic. The ship's own sensors

35

Right:
Near the end of their lives, the remaining 'County' class played a prominent role in the Falklands conflict. HMS *Antrim*, pictured here, led the recapture of South Georgia. *Crown Copyright*

Below:
HMS *Fife* at speed. The Exocet canisters, replacing 'B' turret just before the bridge, can be clearly seen. *Crown Copyright*

include Type 1022 air warning radar incorporating Hollandse-Signaal equipment and a Marconi aerial, with in addition a full fit of target indication, weapon control and navigation sets. What was not available in the South Atlantic was airborne early warning, which by hoisting a radar into the air much extends cover, particularly against low-flying aircraft. This was a serious deficiency, since alleviated by a 'lash-up' radar in a Sea King helicopter.

Sea Kings are, however, primarily anti-submarine aircraft. The *Invincible*'s normal complement is nine, though more were taken to the South Atlantic. In the same way the five Sea Harriers normally carried were much augmented.

The 'Invincible' class has high standards of accommodation and extensive facilities; there are dining halls, recreation spaces and an extensive library, separate from the sleeping areas. The ship's company of 131 officers, 265 senior ratings and 604 junior ratings represent a great variety of specialisations and skills, reinforced when the squadrons are on board.

Now that all three ships of the class are afloat, a farewell has had to be bidden to the well-loved *Hermes*, flagship of the Falklands Task Force and a ship of great achievement. She managed to embark more aircraft than *Invincible*, her 7° 'ski-jump' to assist the take-off of loaded V/STOL aircraft was equally effective, her communication capacity unparalleled. But she had been around a long time, and neither men nor aircraft were on present plans sufficient to keep her operational. At the time of writing she remains in reserve.

Destroyers
The Royal Navy has not been very precise in the way it categorises its medium-sized surface ships. Since the term frigate was reintroduced at the end of World War 2 and the word destroyer retained, it has been hard to distinguish between the two, particularly as both sorts of ships became progressively larger and frequently leap-frogged in size. However, it can be said that as understood by the Navy, destroyers have a primary air defence role and frigates a primary anti-submarine role.

The 'County' Class
The first generation of ships designed to deploy air defence missile systems was a class of 5,400-ton vessels named after British counties, of which in 1984 two were still in the fleet. They came into commission between 1963 and 1970. They are, by common consent, among the handsomest warships ever built, with superb lines tapering towards the stern and well-proportioned superstructure and funnels. Bigger than many prewar cruisers, they are powered by a composite plant of two steam and four gas turbines. Gas turbine boost allows a quick getaway but, in this early system, there are complexities which are reflected in the large engine room complements of these ships. The total ship's company is 485.

The most characteristic item on the armament is the Seaslug Mk 2 missile. This is a first-generation system in which the missile 'rides' to its aircraft target up a beam designated by the associated Type 901 radar. Surface targets within the horizon can also be engaged. Although two 'County' class ships were employed in the South Atlantic conflict, no successful Seaslug engagements were claimed.

Originally, the 'County' class mounted four 4.5in guns in twin mountings. In the remaining ships 'B' mounting has been replaced by four Aerospatiale Exocet MM38 surface-to-surface missiles. These, the shipborne version of the airborne

AM39 used so effectively by Argentina in the South Atlantic, were mounted first in HMS *Norfolk* as the lead ship for the system in the Royal Navy, where it is now widely fitted. The missile, 17ft (5.2m) long and weighing 16.7lb (735kg), is contained in a sealed canister, requiring only user checks when on board. Before firing, it is fed with a designated target position. After launch, during which the launcher must point within 30° of the target's bearing, the missile settles under inertial guidance on a course which will bring it to the target area. It flies at a sea-skimming altitude under the influence of a radar altimeter. At a given distance from the target position, its active radar seeker is switched on and on detecting the target it homes in by a proportional navigation system, delivering a 325lb (160kg) high explosive warhead.

The 'County' class ships also carry two quadruple Seacat mountings for close-in air defence, an anti-submarine helicopter, and a variety of sensors including a Type 184 panoramic medium-range sonar, a Type 965 air warning radar, Type 992 target indication radar and Type 978 heightfinding radar.

They have frequently acted as flagships of group deployments round the world. As the South Atlantic campaign showed, they were not built only for looks. Their guns were particularly useful for bombardment, and *Glamorgan* was the only ship in the conflict to survive an Exocet hit. This, for a ship belonging to a class which was considered somewhat vulnerable because of its above-water Seaslug magazine, was remarkable and points partly to the defensive advantages of sheer size and partly to the effect of skilful ship-handling to minimise damage on impact.

HMS Bristol
The class of which HMS *Bristol* was the first and only representative – the Type 82 – was designed to act as an air defence escort of the new generation of large aircraft carriers in the mid-1960s, and died with it. The completion of *Bristol*, however, was valuable in providing a platform for trials of the new Sea Dart and Ikara missile systems, and the ship herself is a most useful command and control unit, incorporating as she does much comparatively modern sensor, processing and communications equipment. She is unusual in two respects: she is the only three-funnelled ship in the Royal Navy, and she has no helicopter hangar.

The Type 42 Class
This is the most numerous class of surface ships in the Royal Navy apart from the 'Leander' class frigates. The ships were designed to provide most of the capabilities of the *Bristol* on a much smaller hull and with two-thirds of the complement. The first Type 42 launched was HMS *Sheffield* in 1971.

The first 10 ships of the class were of 3,500 tons standard displacement and 410ft (125m) long. HMS *Manchester* and subsequent ships will be 300 tons heavier and 40ft longer. The powerplant is all gas turbine. It consists of two Rolls-Royce Olympus, rated at 20,000kW each, for high-speed running and two Rolls-Royce Tyne for cruising. They work through gearboxes to two Stone Manganese controllable-pitch propellers. Electrical power is provided by four diesel generators in two separate auxiliary machinery spaces.

Before the Falklands conflict several publications described the Type 42s as 'tight ships', with little spare room and not much crew comfort, but also as 'stout ships' with plenty of built-in redundancy and damage control features. It might be thought that the loss of *Sheffield* and *Coventry* in the South

Atlantic disproved this view. But there are few simple, clear-cut answers in sea warfare. *Sheffield* was by all accounts surprised by the first Exocet attack of the war, and fire took hold before all back-up systems could be brought into action. *Coventry* was overwhelmed by a concerted air attack which landed three bombs accurately deep in the ship's vitals. Unlike some of the other Argentine bombs, they all exploded. It is doubtful if any World War 2 cruiser would have survived such an attack.

Given such a small sample and such special circumstances, a statistician would be able to prove nothing (or, if one is cynical about statisticians, anything); what is certain is that the five ships of the class to be engaged fought hard, and that their Sea Dart missiles had an effect more important than their eight claimed aircraft kills indicates. This is because the Sea Dart is most effective against aircraft at medium height, and this was one of the factors that drove the Argentine aircraft down to the deck where their bomb fuses were not always effective. The Sea Dart, a semi-active homing missile, supersonic and agile, is an area defence weapon designed to engage crossing as well as approaching targets. Launch and reloading rates are claimed to be rapid; if these are coupled with high reliability they are an important attribute when dealing with co-ordinated attacks. The Sea Dart can also be used against surface targets, probably out to horizon range. As a result of the Falklands experience, a point defence system will be fitted to augment the ships' air defence resources.

The Type 42 class also deploys the Lynx helicopter for anti-submarine, anti-ship and reconnaissance work; a single 4.5in Mk 8 gun in a fully automatic mounting to provide a further channel of anti-aircraft fire as well as shore bombardment and surface action; and a shipborne torpedo weapon system for firing lightweight homing torpedoes against submarine targets detected by the ship's own Type 184M sonar. Other sensors include Type 965R or (not before time) Type 1022 air warning radar and Type 992Q target indication radar. These, with external information, feed into the ADAWS5 computer system in the operations room. This is a highly centralised system and does not reflect the latest technology; as everyone knows, the generations of the computer family succeed one another very rapidly, and a ship with a relatively long life cannot keep up unless its computer system is extensively modernised during its lifetime. We shall return to this theme before the chapter is over.

Frigates

Before World War 2 ended, naval planners had already turned, from the relatively slow, mass produced frigates that had provided convoy escort and anti-submarine support, to a ship with higher speed capable of making the main anti-submarine contribution to the fleet. This was the genesis of a family of frigates beginning with the 'Whitby' (Type 12) and 'Rothesay' classes, carrying on through the numerous 'Leander' class, coming to a peak in the 'Broadsword' class Type 22 and projected on into the Type 23. All these were designed by the Navy's Ship Department; some of the 'Rothesays' are still serving, but only the 'Leander' class onward will be described in detail. The 'Amazon' class Type 21 was a commercial design and its special characteristics will be mentioned at the end of this account.

The 'Leander' Class

In all, 26 ships of the 'Leander' class were completed between 1963 and 1972. The last 10 had 2ft added to their beam to improve internal space and stability, but in fact the 'Leander' hull, with its fine entry and high freeboard, keeps the sea particularly well.

The ships are powered by a proven system of two controlled superheat boilers and two sets of steam turbines giving 30,000shp (shaft horsepower). Electrical power is provided by a standard combination of steam and diesel generators. The ships have twin rudders and are fitted with stabilisers. All these characteristics were in the ships from the beginning. The armament, however, has undergone major modifications during the mid-life refits of these ships. The programme began in 1972 and was due to complete in 1984; the last few ships were victims of the new policy of doing away with mid-life modernisations, announced in 1981.

The first batch of eight ships was modified principally by removing the 4.5in twin gun turret and fitting in its place the Ikara anti-submarine missile system. The Ikara was developed jointly by the UK and Australia. The missile embodies a lightweight torpedo, and is launched in response to a contact from the ship's or a consort's sonar. Missile trajectory is determined by a computer in the ship's operations room and passed to the missile in flight by a radio command link; the missile is monitored by a specialised control radar. At the computed dropping point, the missile is commanded to release its torpedo, which parachutes into the water and starts an autonomous search for the submarine, homing and attacking

when it gains contact. One of the Ikara's advantages is its 24-hour availability. But these 'Leanders' have also a helicopter which can carry depth charges or torpedoes to a sonar contact; and, for close-range anti-submarine work, they have retained their Type 170 'searchlight' sonar and associated Limbo Mk 10 mortar. Such a comprehensive anti-submarine fit left, for the cautious British designers, little room for air defence or surface weapons and this task is left to two quadruple Seacat launchers and two single 40mm Bofors guns. These ships are now so specialised to an ASW role that their utility as general purpose frigates is questionable. None were deployed in the South Atlantic.

The ships of the second batch of narrow-beam 'Leanders' have been fitted, instead of their 4.5in guns, with four Exocet missiles. They also have three quadruple Seacat launchers and two 40mm Bofors. For anti-submarine work they now have a Lynx helicopter. This has meant removing the Limbo Mk 10 mortar, but for close-range anti-submarine attack the ship has two sets of triple tubes – the ship-launched torpedo weapon system – armed with lightweight homing torpedoes, and the control system to go with them.

Finally, some of the broad-beamed 'Leanders' have had the most extensive (and expensive) modification of all. They have Exocet in place of the 4.5in mounting, provision for a Lynx helicopter, and ship-launched torpedoes. Their air defence will be powerfully enhanced by the Sea Wolf system (which is described in detail below under the 'Broadsword' class). This version of the 'Leanders' will, therefore, be able to approach even more severe air defence environments with some

Above:
HMS *Manchester*, first of the 'stretched' Type 42 destroyers.
Crown Copyright

Right:
Genesis of a long and successful line of British frigates: HMS *Brighton*, of the 'Rothesay' class. *Crown Copyright*

Top right:
The 'Leander' hull shows its sea-keeping qualities: HMS *Andromeda* (before modernisation) in a seaway.
Crown Copyright

Bottom right:
A simple, strap-on addition to the armament: 20mm Oerlikon in HMS *Ariadne*.
Crown Copyright, photo by Chief Petty Officer Drew

confidence, as well as keeping a powerful offensive punch both in anti-submarine and anti-surface vessel warfare. But not all the broad-beam 'Leanders' will be so modified, as a result of the change of modernisation policy.

The 'Broadsword' Class Type 22

Originally conceived as a direct successor to the 'Leander', the 'Broadsword' class Type 22 developed into something a good deal more formidable and autonomous. The reasons are complex, depending as they do on developments in weapon systems – both those fitted in the ship and those provided by other units – and the pattern of operations, particularly in the anti-submarine field. The result is a ship designed chiefly for its ability to look after itself in a hot-war environment and for offensive power against both submarines and surface units.

Air defence is the function of the Sea Wolf GWS25 point defence system. This is claimed to be the most advanced so far in the world in meeting the threat not only from aircraft but from tactical aerodynamic missiles. Studies on the system began in the late 1960s; the requirements were quick reaction,

a high kill probability, ability to operate in all weathers and at night, and easy handling arrangements. The fundamental solution adopted was to put all the complex equipment into the ship and keep the missile simple. This entailed telling it what to do throughout its flight.

The operational sequence of a Sea Wolf GWS25 firing starts with detection of the target by one of the special surveillance radars, Types 967/968. These are mounted back-to-back; 968 is a conventional E-band pulse radar for general surface and air warning, 967 a D-band radar whose pulse-doppler mode is specially suited to picking out fast-moving targets from a mass of stationary clutter. When these indicate a target to the Sea Wolf, one of the sextuple launchers slews rapidly to the bearing and as soon as the target is within effective range one or two missiles can be fired. These are quickly gathered into the beam of the Type 910 guidance radar, which is a

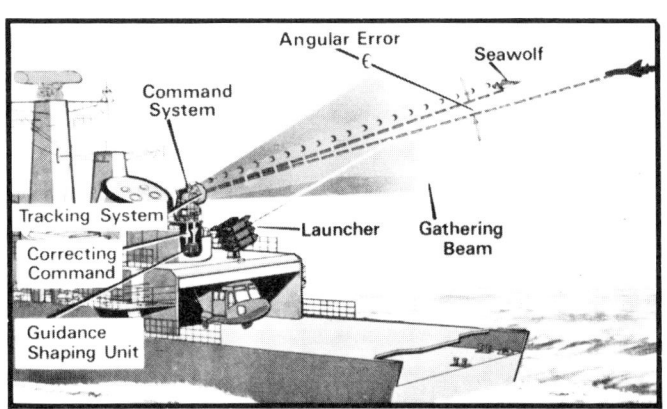

Right:
The principles of Sea Wolf guidance. Angular differences between the missile and target are measured, and the missile ordered to alter course accordingly through a command radio link.
Marconi/Vickers/British Aerospace Dynamics Group

Below:
A potent, but expensive rearmament: HMS *Phoebe* fires an Exocet missile. *Crown Copyright*

monopulse system tracking both the target and the Sea Wolf missile(s) in a time multiplex mode. The 910 measures the angular difference between the Sea Wolf and the target and a command link issues course adjustments so that it closes the target accurately. The Sea Wolf explodes, by proximity or impact fuzing, as it flies by or actually hits the target.

The Sea Wolf performed well in the South Atlantic, five successful engagements being claimed by only three Sea Wolf-fitted ships deployed during the fighting. The number of missiles fired to achieve each success has not been released. Nor has the Sea Wolf's performance against very low flying aircraft. It is unlikely that this was a strong point of the GWS25 system, since it was at that time supplemented by a television tracker – and has since been modified by an additional radar in Ka-band – for such targets. In fact, a radar of this type was available for mating with the Sea Wolf from about 1976, but since it was a Dutch set it perhaps ran into opposition from British industry. But it would be wrong to carp too much about the shortcomings of the first generation of such an innovative system. It is still the best there is in its field, and there are numerous second-generation versions which seek to overcome the limitations of heavy launchers, hand reloading and a very large battery of guidance computers.

The 'Broadsword' class ships are well fitted with sensors in every mode. Electronic warfare equipment gives the ability to conduct signal analysis and direction-finding in the 1-18GHz range; there is navigational radar, and the Lynx helicopter's own radar is a very useful extension of the ship's surveillance reach; and the new Type 2016 sonar is a medium range active set employing very advanced techniques of signal analysis that are designed to provide a better answer than ever before to the question: 'Is that a submarine or not?' All these feed into an operations room that seems to have struck the balance, long

Above:
HMS *Battleaxe*. With Sea Wolf, Exocet and anti-submarine systems, the ship is designed to be capable in anti-surface vessel, ASW and air defence roles. *Crown Copyright*

sought, between trying to tell the command what it should do – and thus stifling initiative – and supplying it with out-of-date and insufficient information – thus giving it no scope to use its initiative anyway.

Command and control is, therefore, one of the class' strong points. But the Type 22 can also take the offensive in many situations. It has four Exocet missiles, ship-mounted torpedo tubes and stowage for two Lynx helicopters. *Broadsword* was the first ship of her size to be gunless, except for two 40mm Bofors, but later units of the class, lengthened, are expected to have a 4.5in Mk 8.

So far 12 of the class have been built or ordered; after the first four (all now in service) the design was lengthened by 49 feet (15 metres) to enhance the weapon fit, extend endurance, improve the already good habitability, and most importantly to accommodate an ASW towed array. The last two of the 12 will in addition deploy a 4.5in mark 8 gun. The Type 22 therefore seems to be running on as the navy's 'quality ship'; a high price is paid for the quality.

The Type 23

Undoubtedly cost was one governing factor in the concept of the Type 23 frigate, sketches and ideas for which no doubt existed before the decisions embodied in the 1981 'Way Forward' document. However these hastened the project, which by all accounts went through many vicissitudes before its official emergence at the Royal Navy Equipment Exhibition in 1983.

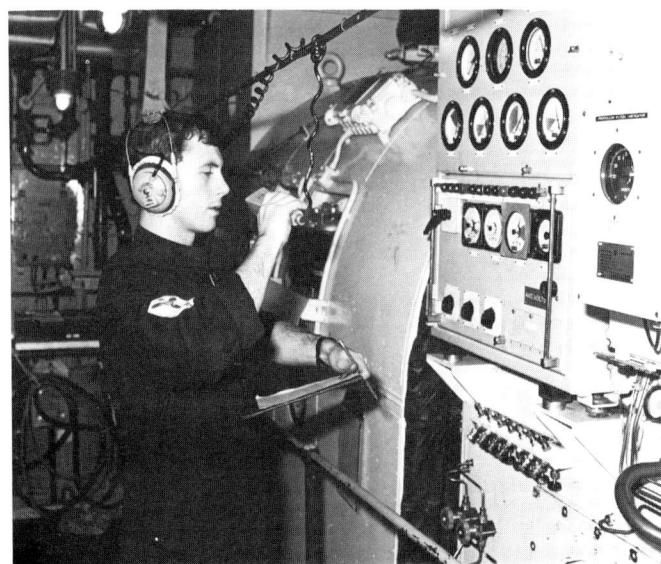

44

Aspects of Life in a Modern Frigate

Far left:
In the Sonar Control Room: visual displays now predominate, but 'pings' still matter.

Left:
In the Operations Room: computers do much of the donkey work, but quick visual appreciation is still important.

Below, Far left:
Main Machinery Space: no steam, but gas turbines need the same attention.

Below left:
Machinery Control Room: not quite the same as 'the plates'.

Bottom, Far left:
Triple torpedo tube for lightweight anti-submarine torpedoes, and owner.

Bottom left:
Sea Wolf loading drill.

Below:
Light anti-aircraft weapons firing. Several more channels of fire have been fitted to each frigate during and since the Falklands operation.

Below right:
Transfer of stores by Lynx helicopter.

Bottom:
Stowing a second Lynx in the hangar. *All Crown Copyright photos, by Chief Petty Officer Smart*

One of the reasons for this troubled genesis was the arrival of an entirely new sensor, the passive sonar towed array. This device made the most of a technical development in anti-submarine warfare that spanned the 1980s and may well dominate the 1990s as well: that is to say, the analysis of submarine-emitted noise by advanced electronic techniques. Hydrophone arrays towed in quiet water a long way astern of a surface ship (or submarine) realised the potential of this system to its maximum. But they were thought to require a rather special sort of ship; or, alternatively, to need only a ship of very limited abilities to tow them. Both these hypotheses seem to have been set aside, and towed arrays are likely to be retrofitted to a number of frigates of earlier classes.

In the event then the Type 23, although it will have the ability to deploy a towed array, is in other respects a pretty orthodox frigate, and a far cry from the very cheap and simple unit originally suggested by some publications of 1981. Its armament is in many respects predictable; a 4.5in gun, eight harpoon surface-to-surface missiles, two 30mm single gun mountings and lightweight torpedo tubes. However, it has two notable weapon innovations: vertical-launch Sea Wolf and very versatile helicopter facilities.

The plans show 32 vertical Sea Wolf tubes mounted at upper deck level; it appears that the Ship Department's previous insistence on deep magazines has undergone a sea change. Details of the system's operation after launch have not been released, but it appears that thrust vector control, operating through swivelling nozzles, will guide the missile into a preset gathering sector where the tracking radar will take it over. Thereafter the process is presumably the same as for the first-generation Sea Wolf, though a specific anti-sea skimming capability is claimed.

Helicopter facilities, including the hangar, will be able to operate not only the Lynx but the Sea King and its replacement, the EH101. This is highly significant in view of the anti-submarine search and attack potential of the larger helicopters, described in the next chapter, and makes every

45

sort of sense when the detection potential of the towed array is taken into account.

Another innovation is the propulsion system. Final drive to the propellors is by electric motors, which reduces transmitted noise to a minimum. For slow speeds the motors are powered by small diesels, for higher speeds by Rolls-Royce Spey SM1A gas turbines. This arrangement, said to be unique and certainly giving rise to a new acronym (CODLAG), is claimed to give a top speed of 28kt and a cruising endurance of 7,000 nautical miles.

More good news on the economy front is the manpower level. The ship is designed to operate with a complement of less than 160, although there is accommodation for 177: 15 officers, 57 senior and 105 junior ratings.

Thus, although not cheap, the Type 23 – the first of which, to be named HMS *Norfolk*, was ordered in October 1984 – does look like a highly versatile ship with a long reach and a strong arm. Its design has been influenced by the Falklands experience and it embodies many new ideas that look good. Everyone will wish it well.

The Type 21

Everyone did not wish the Type 21 frigates well. This class of eight ships was a private-venture design introduced to keep up frigate numbers while the Type 22s were being developed. They had racy yacht-like lines long associated with their chief designer, Vosper-Thornycroft, they used some unorthodox equipment, they were deliberately lightly-built and manned by relatively small complements, and they were bitterly opposed by some elements of the naval materiel establishment.

In fact the armament of the Type 21 is, in offensive terms, both orthodox and powerful for a ship of its displacement. With four Exocet missiles, a 4.5in Mk 8 gun which can carry out a surface or air defence engagement with no one in the turret, and a Lynx helicopter, it is far from being a cream-puff vessel. Defensively, it lacks the more sophisticated air defence systems. The gun is supplemented only by Seacat, with the GWS24 system giving it some blind fire capability, and by two Oerlikon guns. There are thus four channels of anti-aircraft fire, but it is not heavy fire. Self defence against radar homing missiles can be enhanced by the use of chaff rockets which spread metallised strips in the sky to seduce incoming missiles; but this system is common to all modern naval ships. Moreover, it is probably true to say that electrical and mechanical systems on board are less well duplicated, have fewer alternatives, than those of any other RN frigates constructed since World War 2. Finally, the use of aluminium in the upperworks to reduce topweight was bound to increase the potential effects of fire, because although aluminium does not burn it does have a low melting point.

Below:
Artist's impression of the Type 23 frigate. The vertical-launch Sea Wolf installation is between the gun and the surface-to-surface missile system. *Yarrow Shipbuilders Ltd*

Bottom:
HMS *Amazon*, lead ship of the Type 21 frigates. *Rolls-Royce Ltd*

Top:
A version of the chaff decoy: the Shield system being loaded.
Plessey Aerospace

Above:
HMS *Ardent*'s last battle. *Crown Copyright*

All this might suggest that the loss of two Type 21s, *Ardent* and *Antelope*, in the Falklands was predictable. As usual, the full story is not so simple. *Ardent* was in a very isolated position and was made a special target by the Argentine air force – rightly, for she was bombarding Goose Green and softening up the forces there for a crucial assault. *Antelope*, had the bomb within her been defused as were others in other ships, could well have limped home as they did. The other Type 21s in the South Atlantic campaign, and seven out of the eight were in action altogether, were in the thick of things and survived.

What is certain is that this class of ship generates a particularly strong affection in its crews. They are certainly very comfortable, good-looking craft, and the small ship's company makes for added comradeship, but perhaps the reason most of all is the feeling that they are true frigates that will go anywhere and do anything, even if it seems absurdly beyond their powers. I know no-one who served in a Type 21 speak ill of them.

Assault Ships

Of all the ironies of the South Atlantic campaign, none was stranger than the fate of the assault ships *Fearless* and *Intrepid*. Originally designed, with their tank decks and internal docks, to carry troops, heavy equipment and landing craft to far-away areas for amphibious assault operations, they played in their lives a number of roles: ready-made mock merchant ships for convoy training, lifting follow-up echelons for Royal Marines' helicopter assaults mounted from more glamorous ships, and midshipmen's sea training. In 1981 they were due, after a 16-year life, for execution (more or less early, as announcements succeeded one another) under the Government's axe. But in 1982, in San Carlos Water, they did almost exactly what they were first designed to do.

The fact is that these 12,000-ton ships, limited though they are by their lack of speed and of a helicopter hangar, are adaptable and valuable units, giving a great deal of extra potential to a medium-sized navy. They are not yet near the end of their lives and their reprieve is welcome, particularly as their capital cost must surely now be considered amortised. It is, of course, when the time comes to consider replacement that other ideas may be in order.

Arapaho and STUFT

One of the radical solutions for the provision of large-ship facilities is the Arapaho concept, an American idea which takes a fast container merchant ship and, using specially designed and prepared bolt-on equipment, converts it into a vessel capable of carrying aircraft, troops or both. Britain did in effect do this very quickly with some ships taken up from trade (STUFT) in the South Atlantic campaign, and has since leased some more permanent equipment from the USA for fitting in the container ship MV *Astronomer*, now renamed RFA *Reliant*, which is able to operate and service six large helicopters with 150 naval personnel embarked. Another container vessel, *Contender Bezant*, is to be bought and modified as RFA *Argus*.

There are limitations, of course. Damage control arrangements can never be so comprehensive as in a naval-designed ship, and both sensor and control facilities will be less sophisticated than in a warship. Nevertheless, for a maritime force whose operational commitments habitually exceed its peacetime resources, Arapaho must be a worthwhile concept.

The Surface Ship Debate

In the long litany of Words Some People Would Like to Forget is the ministerial statement in a debate (if memory serves right) early in 1981 to the effect that 'had we been planning the fleet now, we should not have included the through-deck cruisers'. In fact, without the organic air capability of the *Invincible* and, of course, *Hermes*, the Falklands operation would have been out of the question, and a deeply shaming outcome of the Argentine invasion inevitable. Nevertheless, the argument over the efficiency of large aircraft-carrying ships is not over. Some people argue that *Hermes* and *Invincible* ought to have been sunk; they are usually the same people who seem to wish we'd lost, and their arguments are unconvincing in the face of the evidence; the ships were not even hit. Others say that no operation of the sort can possibly occur again. The same argument was advanced after Kuwait (1962), the amphibious support of Mr Nyerere's government (1964), the Indonesian confrontation (1964-66) and carrier support of Belize (1977). Its failure rate so far is 100% and there is no reason to suppose

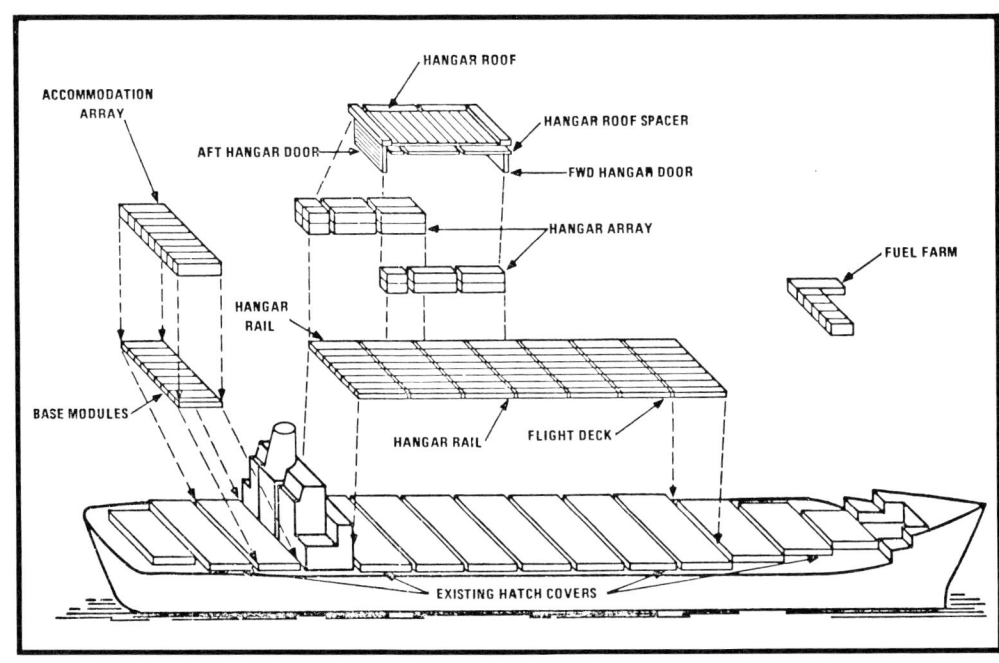

Above:
RFA *Reliant*, formerly MV *Astronomer* and refitted by Cammell Laird Shipbuilders Ltd with the Arapaho system. *Crown Copyright*

Right:
Arapaho: the concept for fitting a container ship to accommodate and operate aircraft. *Navy Department*

HANGAR ROOF

ACCOMMODATION ARRAY

AFT HANGAR DOOR

HANGAR ROOF SPACER

FWD HANGAR DOOR

HANGAR ARRAY

FUEL FARM

HANGAR RAIL

BASE MODULES

HANGAR RAIL

FLIGHT DECK

EXISTING HATCH COVERS

it will fare better in future. Finally, there is a more technical case that the job should be done in a different and cheaper way, by Arapaho supported by command frigates perhaps. 'Perhaps' is the word; the 'Invincible' class was the result of careful cost-effectiveness studies and the country is lucky to have it, in my view.

No, the more rational debate concerns the nature and number of medium-sized surface ships, the frigates and destroyers that make up the bulk of the surface fleet and still take up more of the Navy's procurement budget than any other category of vessel. There are several strands to the debate, of which three may be identified here in ascending order of importance.

The least fundamental, intrinsically, is the fashionable (in 1984) controversy between Long and Thin and Short and Fat. Traditional warship design in all countries has given navies long, thin ships for the claimed advantages of better speed and seakeeping. This design has been challenged, in particular by one British naval architect and his supporters, on the grounds that stability and space can better be provided in a short beamy hull and that speed will not unduly suffer. The arguments are very largely technical and are not appropriate here. What is certain is that the Thin versus Fat debate has got mixed up in the other strands of controversy, for the Fat Frigate is often equated with the Low-cost Frigate. This ain't necessarily so; weapons and systems are often bigger spenders than hull and machinery.

It seems to me that if this technical debate is really important (and it could be, if it is to determine the shape of future generations of ship) then a leaf should be taken from the history books concerning the *Alecto* and *Rattler*, the trial between which in the 1830s settled the Navy on screw rather than paddle propulsion. Let us have a long thin *Alecto*, a short fat *Rattler*, with exactly the same specified operational tasks set by the Naval Staff, and in a prolonged series of independently monitored trials see how they do. This might cost a nine-figure sum; it might be worth it.

The second strand of controversy concerns mid-life modernisation. It was customary in the 1960s to design warship hulls for lives of perhaps 25 years on the assumption that after about 10 years they would go into dockyard hands for prolonged refit and, possibly, transformation. The 'Leanders' were typical examples. Some of their later modernisations were extremely costly, and some of them – notably the Ikara – resulted in ships that were arguably over-specialised in a single role.

There was, therefore, a certain logic behind the 'Way Forward' document's rejection of '. . . costly mid-life modernisations'. But in doing so it accepted that some ships should have their lives drastically shortened, on the grounds that they would be operationally obsolete without modernisation. There never was such a classical case of throwing out the baby with the bathwater. Surely it would have been possible to plan for essential mid-life refurbishment and carefully controlled, trials-proven alterations and additions without altering the character of the ship, and thus kept costs within bounds and numbers of hulls at a reasonable level? It appears from later announcements that this necessary compromise has in fact been reached.

The most important strand in the debate on medium-sized surface ships, however, is the balance between quantity and quality. The Royal Navy has consistently gone for quality: that is to say ships with advanced weapon systems designed for high success rates, ships capable of fleet speed and all-weather

Top:
Simple modifications can add much-needed, if crude, extra channels of fire. *Crown Copyright*

Above:
The 40mm Bofors, for many years a standard subsidiary armament in both surface and air defence roles.
Crown Copyright

seakeeping, ships with high standards of accommodation and crew redundancy to ensure adequate and alert manning of weapons, command, control and information systems for days on end. It has deliberately eschewed the crude and the second-rate, to the extent that the Type 22 had no medium-calibre gun at all because it was thought such guns were outdated.

Such a policy was bound to mean expensive ships, and the Type 22 for example is very expensive indeed; it was £120million a copy in 1981. And there was a school of thought that challenged the quality argument by saying (if I may be forgiven for self-quotation): 'however good their systems, and

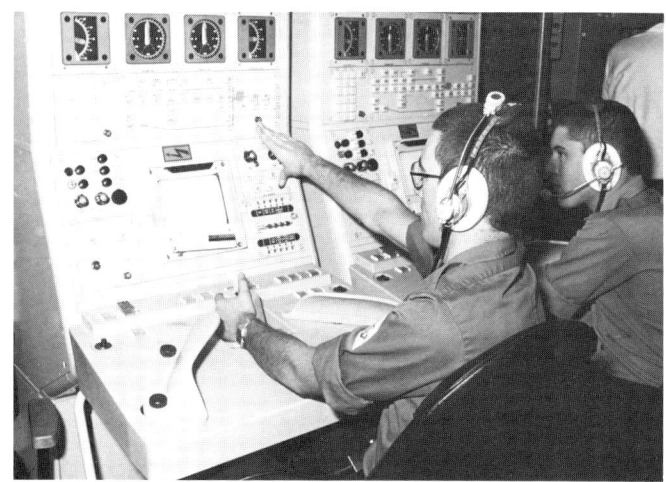

Above:
Sophisticated technology is always expensive, particularly so in systems where there is much innovation. *Crown Copyright*

Below:
Two photographs which illustrate the quality/quantity dilemma: HMS *Birmingham* of the Type 42 class, arguably designed on too tight a budget for a front-line ship; and HMS *Andromeda*, a most expensive high-quality conversion with only a limited remaining life. *Crown Copyright*

however staunch they may be for their size, a good many of them will not survive their first battle, if it comes to that'. This argument is founded on the evidence that in battle, systems *never* perform at their claimed success rates; and that ships of 3-4,000 tons *are* vulnerable to a single or a very few hits. The percentage of such ships that got through World War 2 from beginning to end was really quite low.

It has been said that the South Atlantic campaign gave everyone some evidence to support his own case and that it has changed no-one's mind. Typically: two Type 21s were sunk, so cheap ships are no good; all the Type 22s survived, so expensive ships are cost-effective. On the other hand: two Type 42s were sunk, so sophisticated Sea Dart systems are ineffective; everyone fitted guns on the upper deck, so crude weapons mean something; shore bombardment was very effective, so gunless ships are bad news.

In the upshot, the evidence seems to me to support the view that numbers – both in channels of fire in individual ships, and in numbers of deployable units – have come through as more important than very high planned success-rates in individual equipments or units. Add to that the great increments in cost for an extra few per cent of performance, and you have in my view a powerful argument for reduced sophistication.

There are several important riders to this line of thought. First, one cannot depress the quality too much. The result is a cream-puff Navy that will deter nobody and be brushed aside in conflict. Second, greater numbers of simpler ships may mean acceptance of higher casualties – not necessarily of men (simple ships can have small crews) but of hulls. Third, the Falklands conflict was, as many have said, atypical. Well, all conflicts are atypical, but certainly this one was not against the Russians; it had a very small anti-submarine component, so the evidence in that field is inconclusive though it does seem likely that an Argentine submarine was present for a time and our (high quality) anti-submarine systems did not sink it; and the number of anti-ship missiles deployed against us was, mercifully, small. All in all, the riders do not seem to me to vitiate the case for more relatively unsophisticated ships to supplement the high-quality ones we have already got, and the inception of the Type 23, and thoughts of an even simpler frigate or corvette foreshadowed in the press in late 1983, suggest that that is the direction in which the surface fleet will move.

The British Surface Fleet, 1984

Name and Pendant No		Completed	Length feet (metres)	Beam feet (metres)	Speed knots	Displacement tons	Complement
Anti-submarine Warfare Carriers							
Invincible	(R05)	1979	677	105	30	16,000	670 + 284 for
Illustrious	(R06)	1982	(206)	(32)			squadrons
Ark Royal	(R0?)						embarked
Assault Ships							
Fearless	(L10)	1965-66	520	80	16	12,000	580
Intrepid	(L11)		(158)	(24.4)			
Guided Missile Destroyers							
Glamorgan	(D19)	1968-70	520	54	30	5,440	485
Fife	(D20)		(158)	(16.4)			
Bristol	(D23)	1972	507	55	30	6,000	407
			(154.5)	(16.7)			
Type 42							
Birmingham	(D86)						
Newcastle	(D87)						
Cardiff	(D108)						
Glasgow	(D88)	1976-82	410	48	28	3,500	280
Exeter	(D89)		(125)	(14.6)			
Southampton	(D90)						
Nottingham	(D91)						
Liverpool	(D92)						
Manchester	(D95)						
Edinburgh *	(D97)	1983-	450	50	28	3,850	280
Gloucester *	(D96)		(139)	(15.2)			
York *	(D98)						
Frigates							
'Rothesay'							
Torquay	(F43)						
Rothesay	(F107)						
Yarmouth	(F101)						
Plymouth	(F126)	1960-62	370	41	28	2,450	250
Falmouth	(F113)		(112.8)	(12.5)			
Berwick	(F115)						
Lowestoft	(F103)						
Londonderry	(F108)						

(*Torquay* employed for training, *Londonderry* for trials)

Ikara 'Leander'							
Leander	(F109)						
Aurora	(F10)						
Ajax	(F114)	1963-65	372	41	28	2,650	240
Galatea	(F18)		(113.4)	(12.5)			
Euryalus	(F15)						
Arethusa	(F38)						
Naiad	(F39)						

The British Surface Fleet, 1984 *(cont)*

Name and Pendant No		Completed	Length feet (metres)	Beam feet (metres)	Speed knots	Displacement tons	Complement
Exocet 'Leander'							
Cleopatra	(F28)						
Sirius	(F40)						
Phoebe	(F42)						
Minerva	(F45)	1965-67	372 (113.4)	41 (12.5)	28	2,550	230
Danae	(F47)						
Argonaut	(F56)						
Penelope	(F127)						
Juno	(F52)						

(*Juno* employed as training ship)

Name and Pendant No		Completed	Length feet (metres)	Beam feet (metres)	Speed knots	Displacement tons	Complement
Broad-beam 'Leander', modernised							
Scylla	(F71)						
Jupiter	(F60)						
Andromeda	(F57)	1969-72	372 (113.4)	43 (13.1)	28	2,650	260
Charybdis	(F75)						
Hermione	(F58)						
Broad-beam 'Leander', unmodernised							
Apollo	(F70)						
Achilles	(F12)	1969-72	372 (113.4)	43 (13.1)	28	2,650	260
Diomede	(F16)						
Ariadne	(F72)						
Type 21							
Amazon	(F169)						
Active	(F171)						
Ambuscade	(F172)	1974-78	384 (117)	41.7 (12.7)	30	2,500	170
Arrow	(F173)						
Alacrity	(F174)						
Avenger	(F185)						
Type 22							
Broadsword	(F88)						
Battleaxe	(F89)	1979-82	428.4 (131)	48.1 (14.7)	30	4,500	224
Brilliant	(F90)						
Brazen	(F91)						
Boxer	(F92)						
Beaver	(F93)	1983-	479 (146)	48.1 (14.7)	30	4,850	273
Brave *							
London *							
Sheffield *							
Coventry *							

Two Batch 3 ordered

Name and Pendant No		Completed	Length feet (metres)	Beam feet (metres)	Speed knots	Displacement tons	Complement
Type 23		*(1988)*	*436.2 (133)*	*49.2 (15)*	*28*		*177*
Norfolk							

* Building

5 The Air Component

No part of Britain's maritime power has been so swept by changes in policy, control and resource allocation as its air component. Genuine differences of view on how this should be based, deployed and operated have existed since aircraft first flew over the sea; argued with passion, they have resulted, when compounded with political factors, in several radical changes of command, organisation and structure since 1918.

However, for the purposes of this book it is necessary to describe only the latest of these alterations of course. This occurred in the mid-1960s, when the Government's Defence Review resulted in a decision not to replace those carriers – at the time there were four – that could operate high-performance fixed-wing aircraft. The Review said that the only task specific to such ships was the landing or withdrawal of troops against opposition outside the range of land-based strike aircraft; no such operations were envisaged without allies and the requirement was accordingly to lapse.

There were, however, other tasks attributable to the aircraft of the fixed-wing carriers and these needed to be reallocated. Like all the other plans of the late 1960s, this reallocation was dominated by the NATO task. The solution arrived at, after considerable discussion and adjustment, was that in the deep field, some hundreds of miles from a group of ships requiring air cover, the responsibility of air defence and anti-surface ship strike would rest with Royal Air Force aircraft operating from bases in the United Kingdom, and (as before) anti-submarine air cover in that area would be provided by long-range maritime patrol aircraft of the RAF. Nearer the centre of a sea force, the brunt of anti-submarine air operations would be taken by shipborne helicopters; and anti-ship and air defence would depend on shipborne resources. There was, clearly, scope for considerable overlap between the deep and close fields, but this was fully in accord with the ideas of inter-service co-operation and of defence in depth. There was, equally clearly, a need for a platform to deploy the larger anti-submarine helicopters and to exert on-the-spot control of operations, and as we have seen this evolved into the 'Invincible' class.

There was still a difficulty in the above-water field. Royal Air Force resources, charged also with the air defence of the United Kingdom, were likely to find themselves hard pressed;

Below:
'The V/STOL fixed-wing aircraft . . . emerged as one requirement . . .' A Sea Harrier takes off from HMS *Invincible*'s ski-jump. *Crown Copyright*

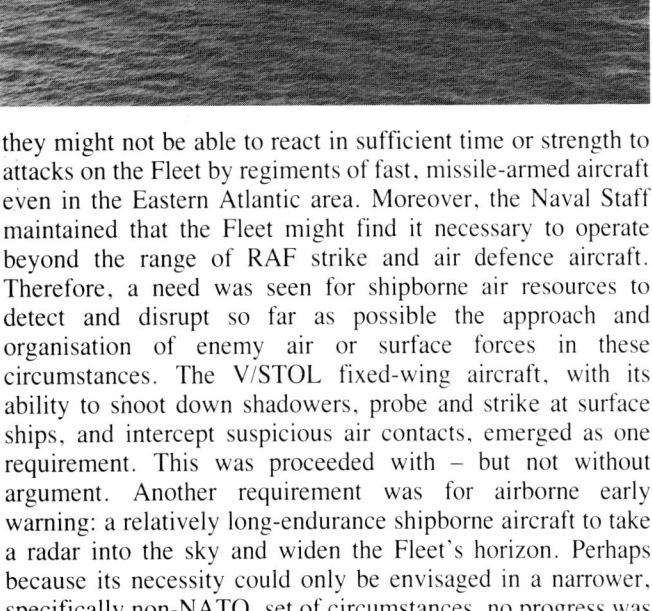

they might not be able to react in sufficient time or strength to attacks on the Fleet by regiments of fast, missile-armed aircraft even in the Eastern Atlantic area. Moreover, the Naval Staff maintained that the Fleet might find it necessary to operate beyond the range of RAF strike and air defence aircraft. Therefore, a need was seen for shipborne air resources to detect and disrupt so far as possible the approach and organisation of enemy air or surface forces in these circumstances. The V/STOL fixed-wing aircraft, with its ability to shoot down shadowers, probe and strike at surface ships, and intercept suspicious air contacts, emerged as one requirement. This was proceeded with – but not without argument. Another requirement was for airborne early warning: a relatively long-endurance shipborne aircraft to take a radar into the sky and widen the Fleet's horizon. Perhaps because its necessity could only be envisaged in a narrower, specifically non-NATO, set of circumstances, no progress was made with this requirement until mid-1982.

Typical Maritime Air Operations
Something that aircraft do very well is **Surveillance, Reconnaissance and Warning** because, as already explained, they have wide horizons. It is also something that combat aircraft need – often from a source outside themselves – because things happen very fast in the air and information is vital. The information can be on air and surface targets – gained mostly by radar, though the eye can help – and also on submarines, mostly through the medium of sonobuoys. The ideal reconnaissance aircraft is roomy and of long endurance.

Probe is a subset of reconnaissance; it is an investigation by air to establish the character of a particular target and usually entails flying close enough for positive identification. Against a heavily-defended target a fast and agile aircraft is needed for probe.

Above left:
Surveillance: a Nimrod Mk 2 of the Royal Air Force.
Crown Copyright

Above:
Probe and air defence: Sea Harriers intercept a Soviet 'Bear' aircraft. *Crown Copyright*

Right:
The Lynx, a multi-role helicopter capable of both anti-submarine warfare and attack on light surface units. *Crown Copyright*

Attack on Surface Vessels may be carried out by missiles, bombs or torpedoes; in modern times, against heavily defended targets, that is definitely the preferred order. Aerodynamic missiles with ranges in excess of 100 miles will leave the parent aircraft relatively unconcerned about any defences except fighters or outlying picket ships. But the longer the release range, the greater the chances of the missile itself being shot down, or going for the wrong target either by accident or through the opponent's countermeasures.

Air Defence has much the same characteristics over the sea as over the land, but over the sea control may be marginally easier, whether for a shipborne or airborne controller or for the fighter itself. For shipborne aircraft flown off the deck at an alert, rates of climb and endurance and range of engagement are all likely to be critical, and if enough aircraft are available combat air patrols are a surer method. But this may apply equally to land-based aircraft in many situations.

Anti-submarine operations are of critical importance to the use of the sea. Any operation against an individual submarine falls into the sequence detection-classification-localisation-tracking-kill. These may all be carried out by one unit, but it is

54

more likely that several units will be employed either sequentially or in co-operation. The sensors used will mostly be acoustic; sonobuoys can be passive or active, dipping sonar (which only helicopters can deploy) is usually active. Anti-submarine weapons will be either depth charges or homing torpedoes. The importance of aircraft in denying the surface – even to the extent of making periscope observations hazardous – is too often forgotten.

Shipborne Aircraft

Small Ships' Helicopters

The first generation small ship's helicopter for the Royal Navy was the Wasp HAS Mk1, carried in frigates and similar ships since 1964. Simple and handy, but with relatively short endurance and only a single engine, it served the Royal Navy well and some are still around. Its chief operational purpose is as a weapon carrier; two Mk 44 or 46 torpedoes can be flown to the area of a submarine contact and, under the ship's direction, dropped close enough to the submarine to enable their self-homing heads to guide them in to the kill. Just how close will be 'close enough' depends on many variables, but from the open literature it appears that it is a few hundred, not thousand, yards. The Wasp can alternatively be armed with anti-submarine depth charges, or with two Nord AS-12 missiles for attacking surface craft.

The Wasp is being superseded by the Lynx, which first flew in 1971 and went into ship's flight service in 1977. This incorporates many innovations including a four-bladed

semi-rigid rotor, sophisticated deck securing arrangements that are very effective in a seaway, and three interconnecting gearboxes which, supplied by two Rolls-Royce Gem engines, drive both the rotors and the auxiliary services. Endurance is impressive for a small ship helicopter; a typical operating profile gives a time on task 50 nautical miles from the ship, with a full anti-submarine weapon load, of 1 hour 55 minutes.

If it is proper to speak of the Lynx as having a primary role, this is still anti-submarine weapon carrying; it can deliver two Mk 46 or Stingray torpedoes, or depth charges. The current British version has no detection equipment of its own so to deliver its weapons it must be directed to the target area by a ship or aircraft in contact. Its impressive array of avionics and communications equipment ensure that this is a relatively simple task.

But the Lynx is nothing if not versatile. It can carry up to nine passengers as well as the pilot and observer who are its normal crew; or up to a ton of internal freight; or, for casualty evacuation, three stretcher cases and a medical attendant. It has, of course, a winch for air-sea rescue. Moreover it can, with its effective radar, greatly expand the surface surveillance of its parent ship.

Finally, however, the Lynx introduced a new dimension into small ship helicopter operations by its combination of the Sea Spray radar and Sea Skua missile for attacking surface craft. The Sea Spray is a lightweight, I-Band, frequency-agile radar optimised to detect and track small surface craft. Its presentation to the observer is made by a specially bright TV raster display which can also show information in a numerical

form. The Sea Skua is a semi-active missile which homes on echoes from a target illuminated by the Sea Spray radar. Its trajectory is sea-skimming and its operation all-weather. It delivers a 44lb (20kg) warhead: not large, but a Lynx can carry four such weapons. The Sea Skua's performance in the South Atlantic was outstanding; eight hits were recorded from eight firings. The ships hit were not always sunk, but were incapacitated.

The success of the Lynx as a multi-role helicopter is indicated by the fact that over 300 are on order, or delivered, in 10 countries; and its potential is shown by the fact that already in some countries' versions it carries dunking sonar, sonobuoys and up-rated engines.

Large Anti-Submarine Helicopters
Deployment of large anti-submarine helicopters in the Royal Navy dates from the mid 1960s. Then, and up to the present day, the helicopters were derivatives of American Sikorsky designs manufactured under licence by Westland Aircraft; the divergences between parent and British design have tended to widen with succeeding generations.

So far there have been three such generations. The first two were the Whirlwind and the Wessex 3, worthy aircraft but hampered by short endurance that made their operating cycles hard to manage and by limited payload that made it hard for them to carry both sensors and weapons – that is, to act as self-contained search and attack systems.

The Sea King, which entered service in 1970, went a very long way to overcoming these drawbacks. It has twin engines, good endurance/payload characteristics, doppler navigation, search radar and homing equipment. In the version standard

throughout the later 1970s, the HAS Mk 2, it deployed a Plessey 195 dipping sonar. The main mode of this set is active. It gives 360° coverage in four 90° steps; bearing accuracy is achieved by the use of multiple beams in each 90° sector. Extensive use is made of the doppler effect – which causes a frequency shift in the echo from a moving target – for classification. The operator can control the depth of the transducer, thus being able to select the optimum depth for the water conditions of the day. Thus the helicopter has the

Left:
The Wasp, first-generation small ship helicopter.
Crown Copyright

Below:
The Lynx, new generation small ship helicopter.
Crown Copyright

Bottom:
The Sea King Mk 5 helicopter, an airborne ASW system capable of both search and attack. *Crown Copyright*

Right:
The Sea Skua air-to-surface missile carried by the Lynx: operational sequence.
British Aerospace Dynamic Group

Below:
A Sea King releases a Sting Ray anti-submarine torpedo.
Crown Copyright

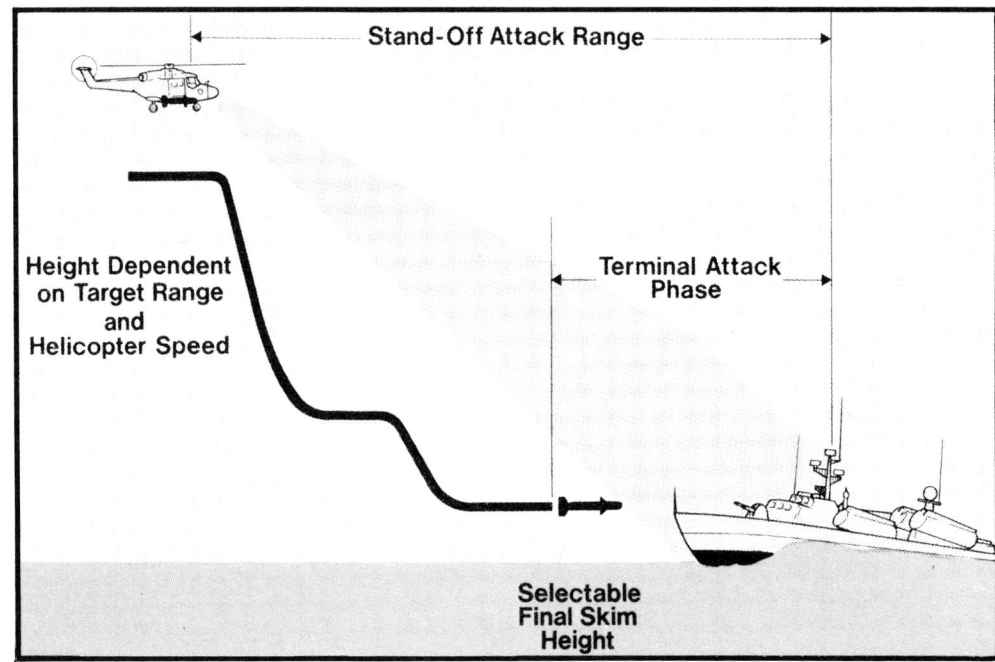

advantage that its sonar is stationary in the water and at the best depth. When it wishes to move, the sonar body is hauled up and the helicopter transits to a new dipping position.

The efficient conduct of both transit and positioning for the dip is the business of the automatic flight control system, developed and built by Louis Newmark. When the helicopter goes into the hover, height and horizontal movement are fed into a computer by a radar altimeter and doppler radar respectively. The computer, working through servos, works the controls so that the helicopter comes to the correct height for dipping and is stationary over the sea. Once the sonar is lowered another set of sensing devices, surrounding the sonar cable, feeds into the computer so that the cable is kept vertical.

All these aids are of great importance when operating a helicopter like the Sea King, which can stay on task for over four hours. The crew – two pilots, an observer and an aircrewman – can save their energies for the time when a contact is classified as a submarine. The Sea King is equipped with weapons as well as sensors and is capable, in the right circumstances, of carrying out the whole anti-submarine sequence from detection to kill.

Weapons now include the Stingray, produced by Marconi Underwater Systems Ltd. This is a lightweight anti-submarine torpedo of similar dimensions to the US Mk 46; but it is an all-British development and is claimed to be half a generation ahead of even the latest updates of the US weapon. This applies particularly to the homing head, which incorporates both passive and frequency-modulated active sonar feeding into a computer whose software, kept up to date as intelligence and experience allow, should ensure that the real target is reliably followed and that false targets – whether fortuitous or deliberately released by the submarine – are rejected. Excellent deep and shallow water performance is claimed, and the computer will even tell its torpedo what sonar modes and attack tactics to adopt once the target is located and classified. Stingray will be carried not only by all anti-submarine helicopters but also by long-range maritime patrol aircraft and in surface ships for firing by the STWS system.

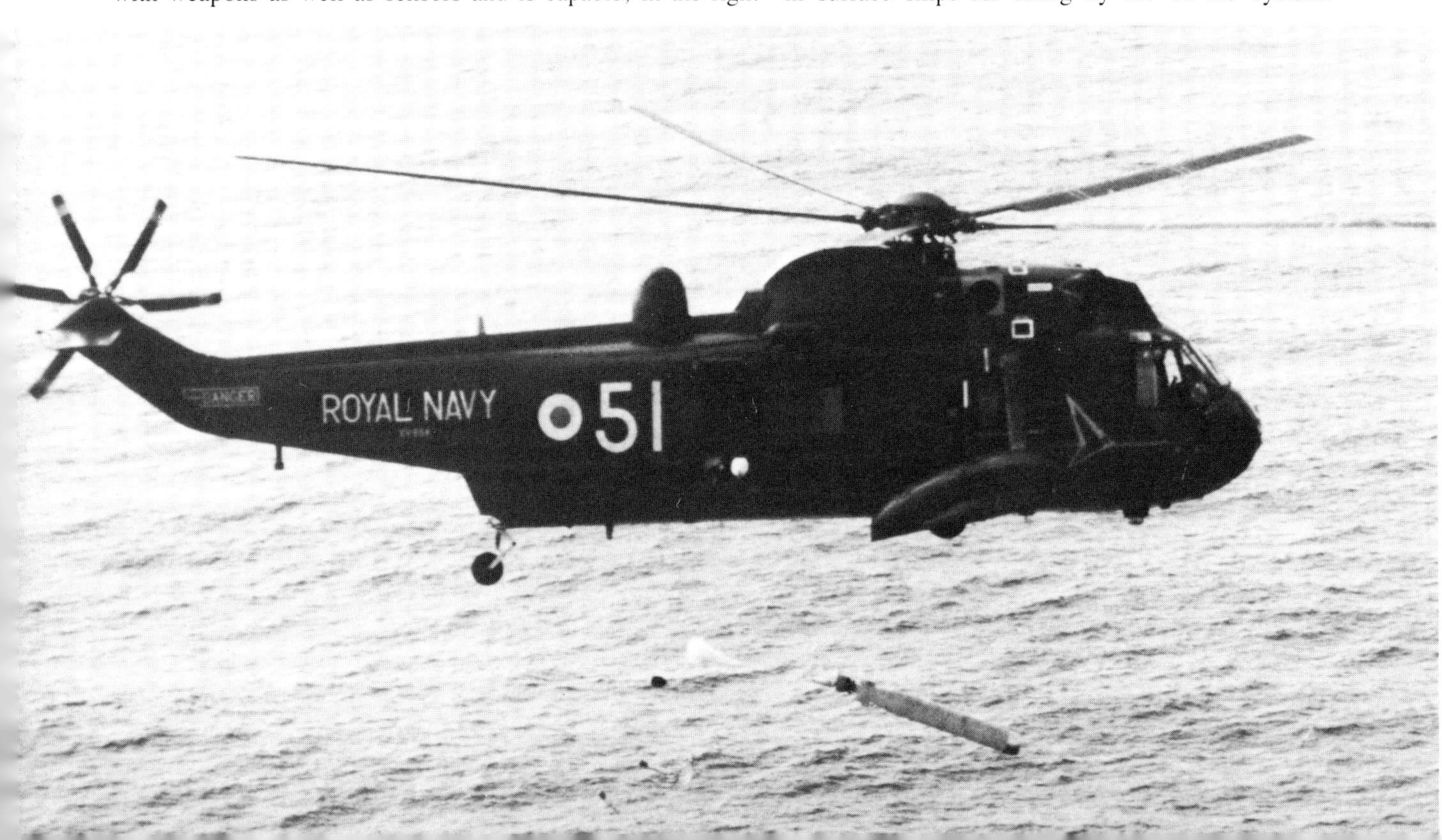

Top right:
Aids and sensors in the Sea King are constantly being improved, and have come a long way from the early installation pictured here. *Crown Copyright*

Above:
A squadron of Sea Kings in formation. *Crown Copyright*

The latest anti-submarine version of the Sea King is the HAS Mk 5. This exploits the very great advances made in the last decade in the detection and processing of submarine noise by passive sonobuoy systems. The buoys used by Sea Kings are mainly of the non-directional variety, laid either as barriers by screening helicopters or as more localised fields to maintain tracking on an already classified contact. They transmit to a multi-channel receiver in the aircraft the noises heard by their transducers. These are fed into analysis equipment using Fast Fourier Transform techniques, which scans the inputs electronically at a very rapid rate. By this means the randomly recurring noises, of each frequency, are filtered out while the consistently occurring ones, such as may be made by a submarine, are retained. The signature thus obtained can be compared with known characteristics of allied and enemy submarines, and can also be displayed both on a cathode ray tube and on 'hard copy' to enable the aircraft crew to set up tracking and attack solutions. Active sonar is normally used only in the final phase of an attack, as is the Magnetic Anomaly Detector (MAD) fitted in the Mk 5. The system as a whole is known as the Lightweight Acoustic Processing and Display System (LAPADS). It is intended that all Sea King ASW helicopters shall eventually be converted to Mk 5 standards.

But airframes do not last for ever, and by the 1990s the Sea Kings will be 20 years old. A replacement is therefore needed, and in logic this should take advantage of developments in helicopter technology since the Sea King was designed. In consequence, the relatively bold step has been taken of moving away from the Sikorsky-based product and embarking on a European helicopter. This, the EH–101, is a joint project by Westland Helicopters and the Italian Agusta company. It is designed as a multi-mission helicopter allowing many variants and adaptations. It will have a crew of three or four and a five-hour endurance, and three engines will give outstanding safety factors and ample power supplies. Avionics and crew comfort will be to the highest modern standards. In the ASW role the aircraft will have a dipping sonar, sonobuoy dispensers and modern, lightweight, high-capacity data processing and management systems, as well as a four-torpedo weapon fit. The helicopter's overall dimensions are rather greater than

those of the Sea King, but the landing gear arrangements should make it handier for deck operation. The memorandum of understanding with the Italian government was signed in January 1984, and the prototype is due to fly in 1986 or 1987.

Airborne Early Warning (AEW) Helicopters
The Government's White Paper on the Lessons Learned from the Falklands Campaign was nowhere more frank than in the passage where it said: 'AEW aircraft could not be deployed at all . . . the absence of AEW was a severe handicap against Argentine air attacks mounted at very low level . . . (and) also proved an important limitation in the Task Force's ability to deal with the threat from Exocet by intercepting the aircraft carrying it before the missile could be launched.'

Of course, the limitation had been well known to the professional Navy for years, ever since the last *Ark Royal* with her AEW Gannets left service. But the re-provision of ship-based AEW could not be justified against the NATO criterion; was not the Eastern Atlantic area to be covered by RAF AEW Shackletons and subsequently Nimrod Mk 3s, and would not the US Navy provide AEW cover to fill any gaps? In theory, yes they would; and so far as the writer knows the requirement was not pressed by the Naval Staff, since it would certainly have been rejected at Treasury level if not before.

Now, however, that has changed. The good endurance of the Sea King helicopter made it an entirely reasonable vehicle for the deployment of AEW, provided that the technical problems could be solved; and in fact this was done at a remarkably rapid rate. Studies began in May 1982, the Searchwater radar was chosen and modified, an aerial and its mounting were designed and made, the Sea King cabin was redesigned to take the processing and display equipment, and the aircraft was test flown and cleared for service by the end of July. Now 824 Squadron has been re-formed and a flight of aircraft will be embarked in each operational carrier.

One consequence must not be blinked. The space required

for the necessary aircraft, on deck and in the hangar, cannot be occupied by other machines. The 'Invincible' class' normal complement of ASW helicopters and Sea Harriers, small enough in all conscience, therefore has to be cut. This need not be critical so long as every opportunity is taken to embark Sea Kings in other ships of a force, support ships and assault ships in particular. It also strengthens the case for the Arapaho concept.

Troop Carrying Helicopters
The first specialised troop-carrying helicopter in the Royal Navy was the Wessex Mk 5. It can carry 14 fully-kitted troops, or an underslung Land Rover, from an off-lying ship to shore. It can also pack an offensive punch, in the event of either small-arms fire from the opposition during a landing or a requirement for support later on; it can carry 2in rockets on pods outside the undercarriage struts, or a fixed forward firing gun in the same position, or a SS-11 missile for anti-tank or anti-strongpoint use. A general purpose machine-gun can be fired through the side door.

There are four squadrons of such helicopters in the latest inventory. As well as commando carrying, the Mk 5 Wessex are used for search and rescue duties at the Royal Naval Air Stations at Portland, Culdrose and Prestwick.

The Sea King has, of course, a considerable load-carrying capacity in non-ASW roles, typically 22 troops or three tons of cargo. The specially-configured utility version, the Sea King HC Mk 4, does even better, with 27 fully-kitted troops or four tons underslung load. One large squadron of such aircraft has been formed and saw service in the Falkland Islands.

The future of troop-carrying helicopters, and in particular how numbers are to be kept up when the Wessex 5 leave service, has not been made clear. It is bound up with the forward plans for troop-carrying and assault ships in general. It

seems almost certain that a full, permanent provision of assault resources for all Britain's amphibious forces will be beyond our means; on the other hand, making no provision and leaving everything to be done ad hoc on the day would be disastrous. The compromise to be reached will need careful discussion.

V/STOL Aircraft
Some aircraft seem destined for an heroic role. The development of the Hawker Siddeley Harrier, against every sort of scepticism and NIH (Not Invented Here) pooh-poohing,

Above left:
The Mk 4 troop-carrying version of the Sea King.
Crown Copyright

Left:
The Sea King shows its versatility by lifting a 105mm gun.
Crown Copyright

Above:
A Sea Harrier lands on during the South Atlantic operations.
Crown Copyright

already showed epic qualities. Its acceptance into operational service, first in the Royal Air Force and then in the Royal Navy, came about mainly because these services could not get the resources to operate the higher-performance aircraft they hankered after in, respectively, the close support and ship-based air defence roles. Operational commanders in both the Army and Navy were perhaps its fairy godfathers; 'I want', said an Army officer of my acquaintance, 'to be able to go out of my tent in the morning and pat it.' Setting aside this notion of the Harrier as a surrogate Labrador, what the services got was in fact the only successful Western attempt to create a V/STOL aircraft with operational abilities; and what they eventually came out with was a war-winner.

The Harrier's propulsion works on a simple principle. A single jet engine transmits its thrust through swivelling nozzles. When they point down, the aircraft goes up, or down

in a controlled manner; when they point aft, it goes forward. Stability during vertical manoeuvres is provided by puffer-jets at the extremities of the aircraft. The technology that turns this principle into practice is anything but simple, but is now well proven.

While it worked on exactly the same principles and used the technology, the Sea Harrier FRS Mk 1 – ordered in 1975 – needed to incorporate some modifications from the ground-based GR3. It has a more corrosion-resistant engine, the Pegasus 104 turbofan, and a raised cockpit for improved pilot vision. Its avionics include the Ferranti Blue Fox radar, which shares many characteristics with the Sea Spray and caters for air-to-air intercept and air-to-surface attack operations. A Head-up Display presents eye-level flight information to the pilot, relieving him of the need to peer into the cockpit. Navigational and communications equipment is of a high standard, and a radar warning receiver is built into the fin. Range and payload characteristics are improved by up to 30% by the innovation of the ski-jump built into the carriers, which gives the Sea Harrier a 'lift' in the short take-off mode.

The Harrier's success in the South Atlantic campaign was outstanding. Sea Harriers were augmented by GR3s of the Royal Air Force, and both types were flown, and performed, brilliantly. With their Sidewinder AIM–9L missiles they shot down 16 Argentine aircraft, and another four with Aden cannon. In the ground support role they kept opposing forces on the jump and did much damage to materiel as well as morale. Their availability was astonishingly high. One must reiterate that as first conceived the Sea Harrier was not

regarded as a fighter to take on opposing combat aircraft, nor as a ground support machine. It was a case of a basically sound fighting vehicle being used to its full potential.

The potential is now to be increased by improvements to the radar and endurance. Moreover, four rather than two Sidewinders will in future be carried, and when it comes into service the British Aerospace Sea Eagle sea-skimming missile, with active radar homing and a high-lethality warhead, will much enhance the Sea Harrier's anti-ship capability. These developments, and of course the replacements for the war losses (six Sea Harriers and three GR3s, all through accident or ground fire) will ensure that the Harrier force remains viable for some years to come.

Shore-based Maritime Aircraft

Long Range Maritime Patrol (LRMP).
Arguably long-range patrol is the oldest of all maritime aircraft roles. Certainly it was the most extensive task of the Royal Naval Air Service in World War 1, when several hundred flying machines were employed in anti-submarine patrols. Between the wars over-confidence in shipborne systems led to

Top:
Royal Air Force Harrier GR3s operated alongside Sea Harriers in the Falklands. *Crown Copyright*

Above:
A Royal Air Force Nimrod Mk 2 long range maritime patrol aircraft. *Crown Copyright*

neglect of maritime patrol aircraft, and it was not until World War 2 was into its fourth year that really effective, very long range aircraft were deployed. They were one of the critical factors in the dramatic turnabout in the Battle of the Atlantic between February and May 1943.

The Royal Air Force has never since then neglected the potential of LRMP, even though it lacked the glamour of the fast combat aircraft. The Shackleton was for many years the mainstay of the LRMP force, but in the late 1960s it was succeeded by the jet-powered Comet derivative, Nimrod. Four squadrons of this aircraft in its Mk 2 version now provide Britain's shore-based anti-submarine potential.

It is an impressive search and weapon system. The central processor is the operational heart of the aircraft; it is the

Marconi AQS-901, a digital processing and display system that is exceptionally clear in presentation as well as quick and accurate in operation. Navigational input comes from the Tactical Aircraft Navigation System (TANS), into which waypoints can be inserted, greatly facilitating the execution of searches and patrols. (The Mk 5 Sea King helicopters have this system too, and find it a great boon.) The sonobuoy inputs are very well presented for analysis in both cathode-ray and hard-copy versions, and can then be transferred automatically to the tactical display for plan presentation, localisation, tracking and attack.

Sonobuoys carried include, as well as the non-directional passive Jezebel, the Barra directional passive buoy developed in Australia; the non-directional active buoy Ranger; and the new directional command-activated multi-beam sonobuoy (CAMBS) whose transducer depth can be varied by command from the aircraft. MAD can be used to confirm classification. But the pride of the sensor suite is probably the Searchwater radar. Very accurate and sensitive, it gives impressively detailed information on the presence, position, size and inclination of surface targets down to submarine periscopes.

The crews of these aircraft are clearly delighted with what they have got, particularly now that in-flight refuelling facilities are fitted to extend the range. There are limitations, of course, particularly at the attack end of the ASW sequence where things are happening very fast and the necessary accuracy depends on everything being right. One sonobuoy giving inconsistent information can spoil one's entire day.

Other Shore-Based Aircraft

For the purposes of maritime air defence, anti-shipping strike, and airborne early warning, and for in-flight refuelling to support those functions, the Royal Air Force can call on a variety of aircraft based in the UK. The figures in the 1983 Statement on the Defence Estimates show four strike/attack squadrons, eight air defence squadrons, one AEW squadron and three tanker squadrons. The aircraft types available include Tornado, Buccaneer, Lightning, Phantom, Shackleton (shortly to be replaced by Nimrod Mk 3) and Victor (to be supplemented by VC-10).

However, it must be remembered that the calls on these resources extend far beyond the support of Britain's maritime effort. They include the air defence of the United Kingdom, operations in support of the Northern Flank and the Baltic Approaches, deployment of Allied Command Europe's Mobile Force, and possibly support of the Central Front itself. With

British Maritime Aircraft, 1984

Type	Wingspan/rotor dia feet (metres)	Length (rotors turning) feet (metres)	Max speed knots	Endurance (hours, normal deployment)	Squadron Nos
Long Range Maritime Patrol					
Nimrod Mk 2	114.8 (35.0)	126.7 (38.6)	500	12	42, 120, 201, 206
ASW Helicopter					
Sea King Mark 5	62.0 (18.9)	72.7 (22.2)	144	4½	706, 810, 814, 819, 820, 826
Multirole Helicopter					
Lynx	42.0 (12.8)	49.7 (14.9)	160	2	702, 815, 35 ships' flights
Wasp	40.0 (12.2)	32.2 (9.8)	120	1¼	829, 32 ships' flights
Troop Carrying Helicopter					
Wessex 5	56.0 (17.1)	65.6 (20.0)	115	2½	707, 845
Sea King Mk 4	62.0 (18.9)	72.7 (22.2)	144	4½	846
AEW					
Nimrod Mk 3	114.8 (35.0)	129.0 (39.3)	500	12	8
Sea King	62.0 (18.9)	72.7 (22.2)	120	4½	824
VSTOL					
Sea Harrier	24.9 (7.6)	46.9 (14.3)	650+	1½	800, 801, 899
Search and Rescue					
Sea King (RAF)	62.0 (18.9)	72.7 (22.2)	144	4½	202
Wessex 5 (RN)	56.0 (17.1)	65.6 (20.0)	115	2½	771, 772
Training					
Gazelle	34.1 (10.4)	34.5 (11.8)	160	1	705

Above:
The shore-based Nimrod 3 airborne early warning aircraft.
Crown Copyright

Below:
The Gazelle, used for basic helicopter training in the Royal Navy and also (in this picture) by the 'Sharks' aerobatic team.
Crown Copyright

the best will in the world, the allocation of sufficient assets in sufficient time to ensure success against maritime threats, in the stress of conflict, is by no means guaranteed. Moreover, in spite of the proximity of the respective fleet and air headquarters at Northwood and High Wycombe, command and control in such circumstances has never been easy. Frequent exercise and flexible procedures are needed to keep it in trim.

Bases

This chapter would not be complete without a mention of the shore stations that serve both the Royal Navy and the Royal

Air Force's maritime effort. However focussed on the sea air forces may be, they need a comprehensive shore organisation for training, administration and technical back-up.

HMS *Heron* at Yeovilton, Somerset is the centre of Fleet Air Arm activity. It is the headquarters of the Flag Officer, Naval Air Command, and the parent station of Sea Harrier and troop-carrying helicopter squadrons.

HMS *Seahawk* at Culdrose, Cornwall is the parent station for Sea King ASW helicopters and the AEW variants, and is the training school for their pilots and all observers. The station also has a very large search and rescue task, covering up to 200 miles out into the Atlantic.

HMS *Osprey* at Portland, Dorset incorporates a naval air station which is the parent for Wasp and Lynx ships' flights and also provides helicopters for a multitude of tasks connected with the Flag Officer, Sea Training's work-up organisation.

HMS *Daedalus* at Lee-on-the-Solent, Hampshire and **HMS** *Gannet* at Prestwick, Scotland are small and specialised establishments, the former training air mechanics and operating local helicopter flights, the latter accommodating Sea King helicopters working with submarines out of Faslane and providing search and rescue cover for the west coast of Scotland.

RAF Kinloss and **St Mawgan,** in Eastern Scotland and Cornwall respectively, are Nimrod bases. The aircraft carry out patrols over the UK's fishing and offshore oil and gas-producing areas in addition to ASW patrols and training. RAF St Mawgan is the training base for Nimrod crews.

RAF stations that might provide other assets for use in maritime roles are too numerous to mention individually, but the bases at Leuchars, Lossiemouth and Brawdy have particularly strong maritime associations.

6 The Royal Marines

The Royal Marines trace their history back to the raising of the Admiral's Regiment in 1664. In over three centuries of sea soldiering there are few things that Corps has not done and few places where it has not been. As early as the reign of George IV, so numerous were its battle honours that over 100 were cited to the King as worthy of inclusion on their colours; that monarch, with one of the happy short cuts of which he was sometimes capable, decreed the device of a globe surrounded with laurel, the motto *Per mare per terram* and the single word 'Gibraltar': a commemoration of the matchless siege of 1704 and a symbol of rock-like steadiness under fire.

The fire has not always come from the enemy. The very variety and scope of the Royal Marines' activities, down the centuries, often led critics to suggest that they had no rational role ashore or afloat, and that all their tasks could be done better by other organisations. The critics' logic would have appeared sounder had it not been for the Royal Marines' extraordinary effectiveness in everything they undertook. It is no surprise that they survive today as a Corps of rather under 7,000 men.

The Commando Role

The Commando idea evolved in World War 2 as a means of providing forces to spearhead attacks and secure lodgments for other forces to exploit. If there is a guiding principle of commando work, it is that of special training to overcome every conceivable sort of obstacle. One obstacle is the enemy, of course. Others may be the sea, rivers, cliffs, mountains, and climatic conditions, and all these have defeated or frustrated military forces before now. In their special preparation to overcome such obstacles, commando-trained forces are following the lead of the first Commandos, those Boer farmers who made such formidable light forces in the war of 1900-02.

It is entirely in keeping with the history of the Royal Marines, including their employment as Commandos in World War 2 itself, that they should have inherited the responsibility for keeping the commando idea alive in all its versatility and adaptability. In the 1950s and 1960s this was often seen east of Suez, as for example in the Suez affair itself, in the Confrontation with Indonesia, and in saving Mr Nyerere's government in Tanzania. But as their role in these so-called 'brush-fire operations' receded (or was thought to recede), so a new task appeared in NATO. The flanks are vulnerable; in Norway, particularly, NATO forces on the ground are desperately outnumbered. Natural obstacles too abound: a deeply indented coastline, rocky terrain, sub-zero temperatures and deep snow in winter, slush, mud, and mosquito-breeding daylight in summer. In such conditions well-acclimatised and highly trained light forces are needed, and those nearest to hand are those based in the United Kingdom. Others may come later, but it is the Royal Marines who would be decisive in helping to blunt or delay an aggressor's advance from the border. The certainty that they are available to give such aid is, of course, a powerful deterrent to any Soviet adventure in the north, and an important encouragement to an exposed and vulnerable ally.

While this is the Royal Marines' primary role in NATO, their training is not over-specialised, and they have in the last two decades exercised in nearly conceivable environment, NATO's Southern Flank and the Baltic approaches being simply two examples. As for the area beyond NATO, in spite of its unfashionable image among the sophisticates of Whitehall, the Royal Marines kept it in mind: with what results, time was to tell.

Organisation and Training

The Commandant-General of the Royal Marines, a lieutenant-general RM, has his headquarters in London and is backed by a small staff. Under him the Royal Marines divide into two organisations each commanded by a major-general: MGRM Commando Forces with his headquarters at Mount Wise in Plymouth, and MGRM Training and Reserve Forces with his headquarters at Eastney, Portsmouth.

Below:
Individual Commando skills.
Crown Copyright, photo by Chief Petty Officer Drew

MGRM Commando Forces has command of 3 Commando Brigade Royal Marines, which as well as headquarters and supporting units consists of 40 Commando, based at Norton Manor Camp, Taunton; 42 Commando, at Bickleigh, Plymouth; and 45 Commando Group, at Arbroath, Scotland. Each Commando consists of about 650 Royal Marines under a lieutenant-colonel RM. Organisation is into companies and troops on orthodox infantry lines, and infantry skills are the basis of the Commando's fighting qualities. The rifle companies hold weapons up to and including general purpose machine guns (GPMG) and 51mm mortars; the support company has a 81mm mortar troop, a MILAN anti-tank troop, an assault engineer troop, a sniper section and a reconnaissance troop. Basic vehicles and communications equipment are to normal infantry scales.

Special to the Royal Marines, however, are a number of skills and equipments. Most strikingly, the Brigade headquarters, 45 Commando Group, 42 Commando and their supporting elements are fully equipped and trained for arctic warfare. They can ski, fight and – more important than anything else – survive in the conditions expected in the Norwegian north and frequently exercise there. They are equipped with Volvo BV202 articulated over-snow vehicles, which are known as 'Bandwagons'. Power is transmitted to the tracks of both components so that, as a colleague said succinctly, if the front can't pull the chances are that the back can push. The vehicle can also tow a light gun.

Under 3 Commando Brigade come a number of other units. Brigade Headquarters and the Commando Logistic Regiment are arctic warfare trained, so that a fully-supported two-Commando arctic deployment is feasible. 59 Independent Commando Squadron Royal Engineers includes specialised

vehicles for beachwork and bridging. 29 Commando Light Regiment, Royal Artillery, is fully integrated into commando skills, as is 148 Commando Forward Observation Battery RA. A raiding squadron attached to 3 Commando Brigade operates both rigid and inflatable craft, and the Brigade has its own helicopter squadron of Gazelle and Lynx aircraft.

Commando Forces have a very close relationship with the Royal Netherlands Marine Corps, from which 1 Amphibious Combat Group and W Company form part of the UK/Netherlands Combined Landing Force. These units are trained and equipped for operations in Norway in winter. This fine Corps, with traditions as long and distinguished as the Royal Marines themselves, makes a full contribution to NATO flank support in skill and hardihood. They train often alongside 45 Commando Group at Arbroath. At Arbroath also is the recently-formed Comacchio Group Royal Marines, specially trained in tasks in connection with the protection from terrorist attack of offshore gas and oil installations.

The MGRM (Training, Reserve and Special Forces) has no less diverse responsibilities. Under him come the two main training centres of the Royal Marines, the Royal Marines School of Music, and the important administrative, secretarial and recruiting organisations which are run from Royal Marines Eastney. He is also responsible for the Royal Marines Reserve, all volunteers and numbering some 1,000 men.

The Commando Training Centre Royal Marines is at Lympstone, Devon. Here every Royal Marine recruit, except buglers and musicians, does a 32-week course in the full range of commando skills. Young officers do a year's training, including the full Commando course. On completion of the course, and not before, a man may wear the green beret. He then generally joins a Commando or headquarters unit, though some, such as clerks and cooks, go straight on to further training for their specialist tasks. There are departments for assault engineer and follow-up weapon training; those needing to be trained in the heavier weapons go to Army establishments. At Lympstone, also, are run the NCOs' courses, and the Physical Training School is here too. Finally, Lympstone is the centre of drill training in the Royal Marines, under the Corps Adjutant and drill instructors. In all these areas of training the very highest standards are set.

Royal Marines Poole, in Dorset, has three main functions.

Left:
Helicopter-borne assault has long been an integral part of Royal Marines training. Sea King and Wessex 5 (airborne) are both shown here. *Crown Copyright*

Below:
The BV202 articulated over-snow vehicle, with unaccustomed driver. *Crown Copyright*

Above:
Infantry skills form the basis of Royal Marines training.
Crown Copyright

First, it trains landing craft handlers, who are volunteers from the rank of corporal upwards, in driving rigid and inflatable raiding craft, and large and small landing craft. Second, it trains ships' Royal Marines detachments which, in certain frigates on (for example) West Indies service, consist of about 10 men, and in ships like *Fearless* and *Intrepid* are a good deal larger. This training is largely to accustom to sea life men who previous experience has been mainly land-based. Finally, RM Poole trains a variety of craftsmen: motor transport drivers and mechanics, carpenters, metalsmiths, printers, equipment repairers. The Joint Warfare School is also located at Poole, having moved there recently from Old Sarum.

The account above has concentrated on operational organisation and training of the main part of the Royal Marines. There are many aspects – musicians, buglers, Special Boat Sections, experimental units – that cannot be covered in detail, for it is necessary to move to an episode where all the organisation and training came together: one that adds significantly to the laurels of the Corps.

1982 - A Memorable Year

1982 began for the Royal Marines in an accustomed pattern and until the end of March went on that way. 42 Commando had just taken part in Exercise 'Alloy Express' in northern Norway, where HMS *Invincible* for the first time had carried a Commando company to lead an assault while still operating in her primary ASW role. 45 Commando Group, after a tough time in Belfast, was in a dispersed state; Y Company was in Brunei for jungle training, Z Company had just lined the streets of London for the Sultan of the same state and then split

up for adventurous training the length and breadth of Europe, and the Commanding Officer was on reconnaissance in Denmark preparatory to an exercise. 40 Commando had been doing similar adventurous training only more so – 782 separate activities having been counted – and had just remustered at Altcar for an Infantry Skill At Arms Competition. Nearly everyone was standing by to go on Easter leave; some early leave parties had already gone.

Naturally this did not apply to Naval Party 8901, the Falkland Islands garrison of some 75 Royal Marines. It was normally half that size; quite by chance the garrisons were turning over when, on 2 April, the Argentine forces invaded. In spite of determined resistance by the Royal Marines, during which several Argentine casualties were sustained, the invaders soon had over 1,000 men ashore and the Governor as Commander-in-Chief ordered the defenders to cease fire and surrender. Much has been made of the fact that the Royal Marines sustained no casualties on this occasion. This book is not in the business of assigning blame, but there are a few points that need to made on this subject in the context of sea power. First, the lack of casualties was due to sheer professionalism: correct use of cover and supporting fire. High-grade troops do not throw their lives away. Second, it did allow Argentina a propaganda, even a diplomatic bonus by parading magnanimity – not too justifiably, since their attack on the barracks at Moody Brook was ruthless and would have resulted in heavy casualties had the barracks been occupied. Third, had British casualties occurred it would have been much harder for Argentina to pretend, while in occupation of the Falklands, that no state of hostilities existed; and later some of the more extreme sophistry about Exclusion Zones and Rules of Engagement might have been avoided. These points do no more than state some of the paradoxes that occur in limited military operations.

To return to the main body of the Corps, it was in a state of

The Royal Marines in the South Atlantic, 1982

Left:
Drills on board *Canberra.* *Crown Copyright*

Below left:
Extensive trials were carried out on the trip south: men carried this much ashore, too. *Crown Copyright*

Above:
Organised chaos on the tank deck of HMS *Fearless* **before the landing.** *Crown Copyright*

Below:
In a corridor of the *Canberra,* **21 May.** *Crown Copyright*

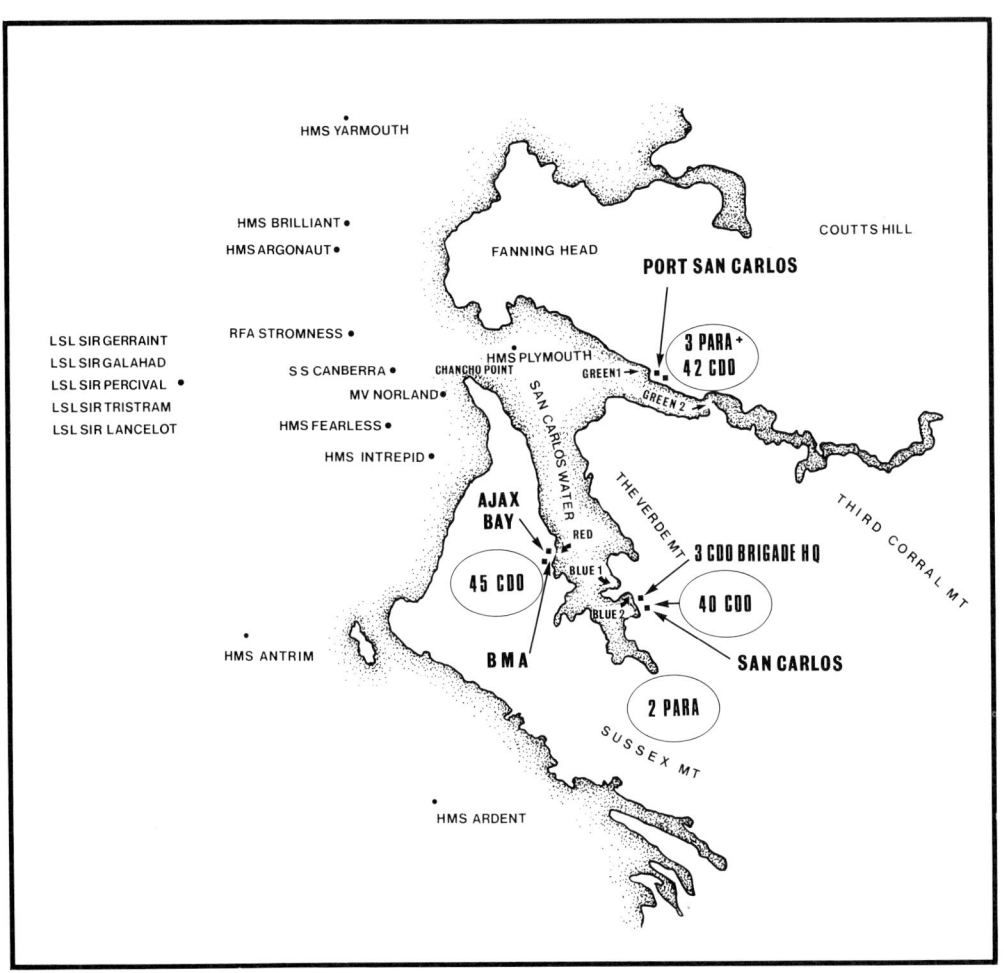

Right:
The landing points.
Globe and Laurel

Below:
The land campaign.
Globe and Laurel

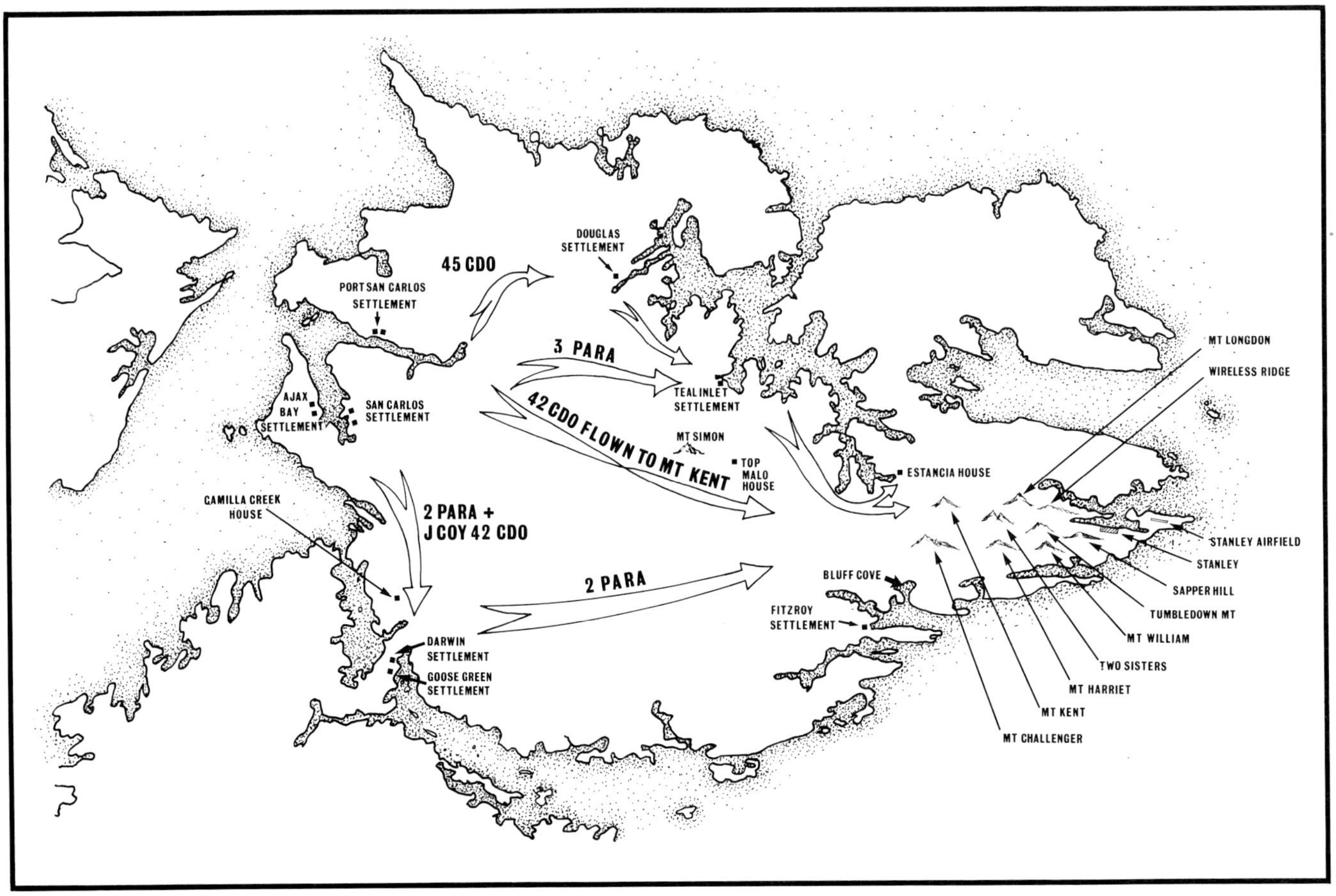

HMS YARMOUTH

HMS BRILLIANT
HMS ARGONAUT

COUTTS HILL

FANNING HEAD

PORT SAN CARLOS

LSL SIR GERRAINT
LSL SIR GALAHAD
LSL SIR PERCIVAL
LSL SIR TRISTRAM
LSL SIR LANCELOT

RFA STROMNESS

HMS PLYMOUTH

GREEN 1

3 PARA +
42 CDO

GREEN 2

S S CANBERRA
CHANCHO POINT
MV NORLAND
HMS FEARLESS
HMS INTREPID

SAN CARLOS WATER

THE VERDE MT

THIRD CORRAL MT

AJAX
BAY

RED

BLUE 1

3 CDO BRIGADE HQ

45 CDO

BLUE 2

40 CDO

HMS ANTRIM

BMA

SAN CARLOS

2 PARA

SUSSEX MT

HMS ARDENT

45 CDO
DOUGLAS
SETTLEMENT

PORT SAN CARLOS
SETTLEMENT

3 PARA

TEAL INLET
SETTLEMENT

42 CDO FLOWN TO MT KENT

MT SIMON

MT LONGDON
WIRELESS RIDGE

AJAX
BAY
SETTLEMENT

SAN CARLOS
SETTLEMENT

TOP
MALO
HOUSE

ESTANCIA HOUSE

CAMILLA CREEK
HOUSE

2 PARA +
J COY 42 CDO

STANLEY AIRFIELD
STANLEY

2 PARA

BLUFF COVE

SAPPER HILL

FITZROY
SETTLEMENT

TUMBLEDOWN MT

DARWIN
SETTLEMENT
GOOSE GREEN
SETTLEMENT

MT WILLIAM

TWO SISTERS

MT HARRIET

MT KENT

MT CHALLENGER

72

feverish activity all over the first weekend of April. Men were recalled, war maintenance reserves of equipment, ammunition and vehicles activated, and loaded – not exactly into anything that floated, but certainly not in a manner that would allow it to be tactically unloaded at the other end. So effective was all this activity that substantial leading elements of 3 Commando Brigade – now swelled by 2nd and 3rd Battalions The Parachute Regiment, various unaccustomed supporting units such as Rapier air defence missile batteries, and two helicopter squadrons – were at sea and on their way south by 6 April, and the remainder followed in SS *Canberra* on 9 April. It was the most remarkable deployment in the history of amphibious warfare.

At Ascension Island, 10 days later, comprehensive restowing of both men and material was begun. The opportunity was also taken to brush up on assault training, and fitness – already a matter for fierce competition, particularly between the Royal Marines and the Paras – was brought to its peak. Spirits were lifted during the period by the news of the recapture of South Georgia by M Company of 42 Commando – a tale that deserves a chapter to itself. When the amphibious force left Ascension on 8 May, all diplomatic efforts at a settlement having long since been exhausted and with the hostilities at sea in full career, it was tactically loaded and ready. The amphibious shipping was an interesting collection: SS *Canberra*, HM Ships *Fearless* and *Intrepid*, MVs *Norland* and *Europic Ferry*, and the landing ships logistic with Arthurian names.

After comprehensive briefings at sea on the landings and follow-up plans, the force arrived in Falkland Sound in the early morning of 21 May and 40 Commando, 2 Para and elements of the Blues & Royals landed at the head of San Carlos Water. Meanwhile the Special Boat Section took Fanning Head against fierce opposition from a company of Argentinians. Two hours later 45 Commando landed at Ajax Bay and established itself on the heights above, and later still 42 Commando, which on board SS *Canberra* in 'bomb alley' had already decided that 'the safest place to be was ashore', arrived with some relief at Port San Carlos, cleared the high ground there of a small force of Argentine troops and dug in.

From there on the adventures of the Commandos must be followed separately. 40 Commando had the least glamorous and most frustrating task, that of defending the base area. B Company in fact remained in this area throughout the campaign, mopping up some isolated Argentinian soldiers in the process; but A and C Companies saw more of the advance to Port Stanley, since they moved to Bluff Cove to augment the Welsh Guards who had just suffered severe casualties in the bombings there. Their assault on Sapper Hill, overlooking Port Stanley, was almost the last of the campaign. The Commando headquarters and B Company then moved to West Falkland to take the surrender of the Argentine forces there.

The men of 42 Commando, having been held in reserve during the initial landings and then made Brigade reserve when they did get ashore, must have been uncertain of their chances of seeing action, but in the event they saw as much as any. They were earmarked to follow up and reinforce 2 Para in the memorable battle at Goose Green, but that terminated before they came into action. Then, however, they were ordered to take Mount Kent, an important feature three-quarters of the way to Stanley. The assault was to be by helicopter, and after an abortive and highly dangerous first attempt in blizzard conditions, was successfully completed with the help of the SAS the next night. K Company stayed there for the next six

Above:
'The safest place to be was ashore' – later on 21 May. *PA*

Below:
Mexefloat and landing craft pass HMS *Yarmouth* in San Carlos water. *Crown Copyright*

Bottom:
Touchdown: for real. *Crown Copyright*

days. Meanwhile L Company leapfrogged to Mount Challenger and J Company – a hastily-assembled unit formed partly of repatriated Marines from the original garrison – carried on to Mount Wall. Then the unit gathered for the culmination of the campaign, the assault on Mount Harriet. This was a classical infantry attack with all-arms support; 42 Commando carried the enemy position from the rear and all its companies had tales of spirit and high courage to tell. It was, as events later proved, the last major and decisive battle of the campaign.

45 Commando was the most travelled of all – on foot at any rate. Others may have 'yomped' much of the time; 45 seems to have yomped all the way. Having established themselves at Ajax Bay, the men moved out on 27 May to Douglas Settlement, on to Teal Inlet and at the beginning of June to the rear of Mount Kent. During all this time they had been tightening the Brigade's hold on the whole of East Falkland; on 10 June the tempo changed with orders to take part in the Brigade attack and themselves to take Two Sisters Hill. X Company attacked the western peak, and two hours later Y and Z

Right:
K Company 42 Commando crosses Mount Kent.
Crown Copyright, photo by Petty Officer Holdgate

Far right:
Essential fire support. *Crown Copyright*

Below:
Lift from Mount Kent to Mount Challenger.
Crown Copyright, photo by Petty Officer Holdgate

Above left:
Mine clearance was essential too.   *Crown Copyright*

Above:
No less important, the tasks of violent peace: Marine Ed Wilson of Support Company 42 Commando on patrol in Crossmaglen.
Crown Copyright

Companies, with the tactical headquarters between them, the eastern. The fight was extremely fierce and the attacks pressed home with great skill and determination.

This necessarily brief account of the three major fighting units' campaign has left all too many gaps, and it is difficult to know which ones to fill. The selfless and absolutely necessary work of the support, surveillance and logistic units – not forgetting the Commando Forces Band, which went too – must be mentioned, as must the brave work of all those who were involved in mine disposal. The raiding squadron went everywhere there was water; and the medical squadron of the Commando Logistic Regiment achieved superb standards of courage, skill and endurance at Ajax Bay, one of the most bombed places in East Falkland. The Royal Marines lost 38 men in a campaign that had nothing easy about it. At the end their spirit was undimmed: as they gathered, dirty and tired, at a pub in Stanley someone muttered 'It's a long way to go for a drink'.

After that, a chapter in a book ought to stop, I suppose. But this is an account of the Royal Marines in the year 1982, and their year went on. After the long voyage home (and there was still PT), the happy reunions, the well-earned leave, the honours and the parades, thers was much work to do

'Re-affirming', as someone put it, '100% fitness for role'. Training in preparation for Norway, for Northern Ireland; reorganisation into more orthodox units from some of those specially assembled; courses for those who had missed them; sport and all the more routine activities of peacetime: all these occupy the time as they did before that strange, remote yet no less real campaign. Nothing could have shown more clearly the results of correctly projected sea power, and the part of well-organised and well-trained amphibious forces in it; and although that was not why it was done, we can be grateful that the demonstration occurred. The Royal Marines have always been great survivors, and even had the South Atlantic campaign not happened their future would have been in little doubt. There should be no doubt about it now.

7 The Offshore Tapestry

The phrase 'Offshore Tapestry' was coined in the early 1970s to describe the public management and good order of the sea areas round the United Kingdom in both peace and war. It aptly expresses the weaving of many strands that is necessary to ensure international order and national well-being.

The International Legal Position

International law already allows Britain sovereign rights for the exploration and exploitation of non-living, and sedentary living, resources of the sea bed and subsoil of the continental shelf around the United Kingdom. Subsequent to the 1983 settlement of the European Common Fisheries Policy, Britain also has extensive rights in the fisheries in European offshore waters out to 200 miles from the coast. In spite of the United Kingdom's failure, for quite inadequately explained reasons, to sign the Montego Bay Law of the Sea Convention of 1982, such rights can now be regarded as customary and general in their application. So can the right to extend the territorial sea from its present three-mile width to 12 miles. In this belt the coastal state has all the rights and responsibilities of sovereignty and may impose traffic schemes and pollution control regulations while still recognising rights of passage; in the areas of resource enjoyment beyond, its rights of regulation will be more limited, but it will clearly, in such a busy sea area, have a profound interest in good order.

Hydrography

One of the very best bases for good order at sea is an accurate set of charts. Since its inception in 1795 the Hydrographic Department of the Royal Navy has set the highest standards; 'Trust in God and an Admiralty Chart' is still in the mariner's vocabulary. The Naval Surveying Service has, since the palm-fringed days when it charted the world, followed the general contraction of horizons, and much of its work is now done around the shores of the UK. There are good hydrographic, as well as political and economic, reasons for this. The North Sea and Channel are the busiest sea areas in the world, and the ones where deep-draught ships habitually work to the tightest depth margins. But depths here tend to be unstable; tides and gales cause phenomena such as sand waves, which can quickly and quite radically alter bottom contours. Even in more remote areas round our shores, surveying effort is needed, for today's remote area may become tomorrow's busy highway.

To carry out these tasks, as well as the oceanographic ones that still demand effort, the Hydrographer of the Navy has a fleet of 11 ships. None are in their first youth, but all are built or adapted to advanced technical standards and they have proved capable of exceptionally swift and accurate work.

The ocean survey ships of the 'Hecla' class displace 2,800 tons. They have diesel-electric drive giving outstanding fuel economy and, with a bow thruster, flexible manoeuvring. Comprehensive sensing devices both above and below water ensure that exceptionally accurate physical and positional data can be obtained. Information is fed into three main processing areas: the automatic plotter on which the ship's position is

Below:
The survey ship HMS *Hydra*. *Crown Copyright*

Above:
The coastal survey vessels *Fox* and *Fawn*.   *Crown Copyright*

constantly recorded together with other chosen data, the dry laboratory where the ship's main computer carries out calculating and recording functions, and the wet laboratory where the properties of sea samples are analysed.

The coastal and inshore survey vessels are not oceanographic craft, so they do not have the laboratories of the larger ships. This apart, they are capable of an equally sophisticated surveying effort. Most surveying ships carry surveying motorboats for inshore and harbour work; even these craft have highly accurate echo-sounders and electronic position fixing devices.

Surveying ships' crews range from about 120 in the 'Hecla' class to some 20 in the inshore craft. When the ship is on survey work, everyone is involved; detachments on inshore work, coastlining or setting up position fixing aids are frequent; and the work is as varied and absorbing as anything the Navy can offer.

Traffic Regulation
Schemes for the separation of shipping traffic into lanes for travel in a certain direction are of comparatively recent origin. In general, their mandatory nature stems not from the state off whose coast they lie – though states are allowed to make schemes within their territorial sea compulsory – but from the agreement of the flag states of ships which use them. Consequently the enforcement of such schemes is generally a matter of informing and warning, rather than directing or detaining transgressors. The Department of Trade, and HM Coastguard as its agent, has an overall responsibility for this aspect of regulation, but air and warship surveillance can be useful and is conducted from time to time as a matter of routine, as well as in specific situations.

Marking of Dangers and Salvage
No less than traffic regulation, these are essential elements in good order in coastal waters. Outside port limits in United Kingdom waters, buoyage, wreck marking and lighthouses are the responsibility of Trinity House, which runs a considerable and efficient organisation to keep them in operation. Salvage is a much more tangled area in which both private enterprise of a rather predatory kind, and some pretty old-fashioned law, are intimately involved. The *Amoco Cadiz* disaster off the French coast showed how dangerous, when unimaginatively handled, current salvage practices can be; it led among other things to the French government making draconian laws that were probably unjustified and certainly set an unfortunate precedent for other states. Some reform of salvage procedures is urgently needed; in the meantime, coastal states will feel impelled to intervene, probably with maritime forces since they are under government control, in case of a marine casualty.

Pollution Control
Tanker casualties are, in the public mind, the most common cause of pollution of the marine environment. In fact this is a misconception; three-quarters of marine pollution comes not from ship but from shore sources. Nevertheless the control of vessel-source pollution is a charge on the coastal state; in the UK it is the responsibility of the Department of Trade, and falls into three categories: first, the prevention of collisions and groundings (traffic regulation, buoyage and navigational aids, and scrutiny in port of ship's equipment and standards of competence all help here); second, the containment of pollution after a casualty; third, the prevention of deliberate discharges of pollutants.

All three kinds of control demand a central co-ordinating body that makes use of many sources of information and of many agents to take action. Not many of the sources or agents will have a primary anti-pollution role; contrary to impressions given in the press, incidents are not frequent enough to justify

78

standing patrols and large specialised resources. But vigilance – particularly from the air – is important, and planning for the best use of ad hoc resources equally so. Within the last few years an organisation for this has been set up in the UK and is frequently exercised, but it has not yet been subjected to the test of a major disaster.

Life-Saving

In the event of marine casualties round the British coast, a variety of agencies may be involved in life-saving: the Royal National Lifeboat Institution, HM Coastguard, British or foreign merchant ships, RAF aircraft, and ships and aircraft of the RN. For many years machinery has existed to co-ordinate these assets, and constant efforts are made to improve its cohesion and response time. Regrettably, as the Penlee lifeboat disaster in 1982 showed, these are not always enough to defeat the most extreme rigours of the sea. Nevertheless in 1983 969 persons were helped to safety by the fighting services alone.

Right:
A notable sea rescue of the 1970s: British and German Sea Kings lifted seven people to safety in this operation. *Crown Copyright*

Below:
A naval fireman fighting a blaze on board a merchant vessel off the coast of Scotland. *Crown Copyright*

Fishery Protection

The Fishery Protection Squadron claimed to be the oldest branch of the Navy, dating back to 1379. It may have been simpler then. It is very complex now, with the various means of conserving fish stocks – catch quotas, close seasons, closed areas, minimum net sizes and licences – at last agreed among the Europeans but still difficult to enforce.

For many years fishery protection was carried out by ships and aircraft designed for other tasks, and to some extent this is still so. Frigates and Nimrods are not optimised for the job. However, the Royal Navy does now have some specialised craft for offshore duties.

The 'Island' class offshore patrol vessels, which came into service between 1977 and 1979, are of 1,000 tons standard displacement. They are trawler-shaped and stabilisers have improved their seakeeping. Two diesel engines driving a single shaft give them 16kt. They have lately been joined by the two 'Castle' class offshore patrol vessels Mk 2, with greater size, better seakeeping and the ability to land on and fuel a Sea King helicopter. It would not take much modification to turn an OPV Mk 2 into a corvette. A fortiori this will apply to the OPV Mk 3, at present a project only for which competitive design studies have been invited from firms. The need is stated to be a capable but low-cost vessel able to undertake a wide range of low level tasks to complement the higher capability destroyers and frigates.

As more modern vessels come into service, the coastal minesweepers still in the Fishery Protection Squadron will be retired or take up roles closer inshore. But their exploits in keeping control of fisheries while still using the minimum of force will long be remembered, from the countless crossings in bucketing Gemini dinghies to trawlers for net inspection, to a famous occasion when a minesweeper ran alongside a

Above:
Naval divers check a North Sea oil platform.   *Crown Copyright*

Below:
The new seabed operations vessel, HMS *Challenger*; this aerial view shows her using her three bow thrusters for an on-the-spot turn to port.   *Mike Lennon*

poaching trawler at dead of night with Wagnerian menace, furiously firing blank Bofors on the disengaged bow and assaulting the trawler's bridge window with a single well-directed King Edward potato. Surrender was instantaneous.

Oil and Gas Rig Protection

The threat to oil and gas installations in the North Sea has been a matter of debate since the early 1970s. Views on it have ranged from the highly alarmist, which sees saboteurs clinging to the legs of every rig, to totally complacent. Whatever view is taken, the chief deterrent must lie in random patrols by watchful and capable units both above and under the surface, and a quick-reaction force that can respond if a threat is found to develop.

Above-water patrols are the responsibility mainly of the Fishery Protection Squadron and of the Royal Air Force Nimrods. Underwater surveillance is often conducted by the oil companies themselves but Royal Navy divers have done training on the rigs and a new seabed operations vessel, HMS *Challenger*, built mainly for submarine recovery, is also available for this task. Finally, quick reaction to a developed threat is provided by Comacchio Group of the Royal Marines, over 400 strong and stationed at Arbroath. Specially trained in rig protection work, using helicopters or raiding craft as appropriate, they would make any would-be saboteur or hi-jacker think several times before making an attempt.

Mine Countermeasures

Mining caused a great many shipping casualties in both world wars, and some in local wars since; and it may well be wrong to place mine countermeasures in this chapter, since they properly form part of the defence of the UK base. Nevertheless they are essentially an offshore task.

The threat is from both ground and moored mines, and there are several ways of actuating either: by contact, by the magnetic influence of a ship's hull, by the noise of its engines,

Above:

All in one piece: the glass reinforced plastic hull of a mine countermeasures vessel under construction.
Vosper Thornycroft (UK) Ltd

Below:

HMS *Abdiel*, a 1,500-ton exercise minelayer and headquarters ship for the mine countermeasures squadrons. *Crown Copyright*

Acoustic minesweeping: the minesweeper tows the Osborn Towed Acoustic Generator (TAG), the cylindrical device on the left, which generates wideband sound. The Towed Acoustic Monitor, the 'winged' body at the end of the other wire, listens to the sound actually transmitted by the TAG so that the ship can, if desired, adjust it to suit varying water conditions. Magnetic and moored mine actuations require different methods of sweeping. All require quiet, non-magnetic, manoeuvrable, expensive minesweepers. *Sperry Gyroscope*

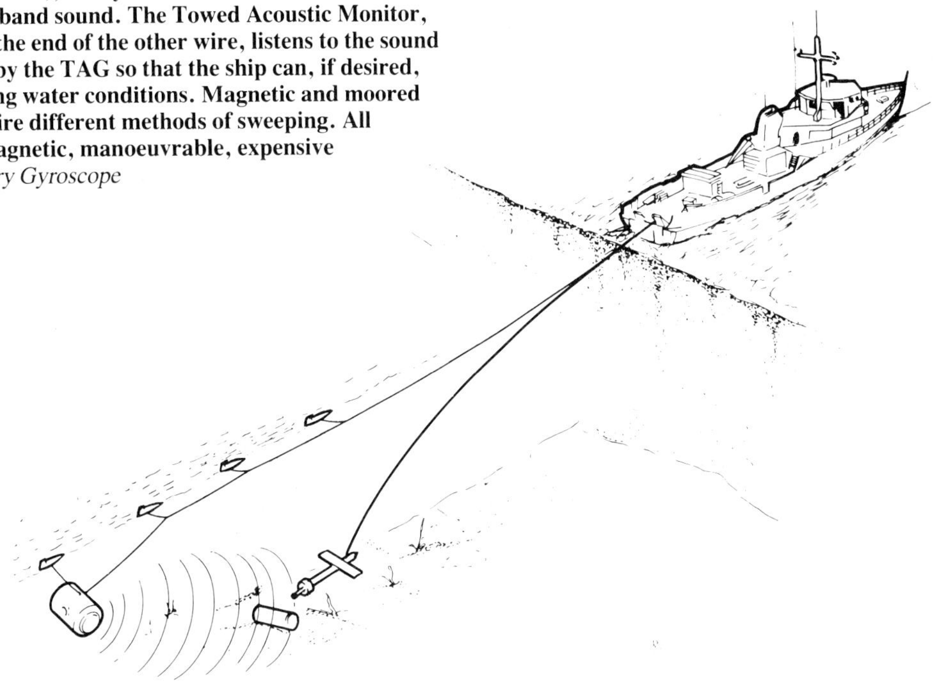

Below:
HMS *Cottesmore*, fourth of the 'Hunt' class mine countermeasures vessels, equipped for both hunting and sweeping. *Crown Copyright*

or by the pressure waves it creates. These can be varied by delayed arming, either by time or by ship-count mechanisms that allow several ships to pass unscathed and then go off under the next unsuspecting passer-by. All are available to the Soviet Union, which has very large mine stocks and many craft fitted for minelaying.

Each arming technique requires a different countermeasure, and moreover it is necessary that a mine countermeasures vessel should have very low magnetic and acoustic signatures so that it will not itself set off a mine before it can neutralise it. The techniques available include minesweeping, in which an abrasive wire armed with cutters is towed to cut through the cables of moored mines; and mine-hunting, where the ship searches ahead of itself with a high-definition sonar, and when a ground mine is detected, stops, investigates and destroys it using a remotely controlled submersible.

The Royal Navy's new glass reinforced plastic-hulled 'Hunt' class mine countermeasures vessels combine both roles, a solution which was developed particularly for the critical Clyde approaches and has resulted in a highly effective, but singularly expensive, ship. For the rest of the immense task round the British coasts, the existing 'Ton' class coastal minesweepers and minehunters, built in the 1950s, have for the time being to suffice; but they will be succeeded

Right:
The diving support ship *Seaforth Clansman*, chartered some years before the South Atlantic operations and retained for saturation diving duties. *Crown Copyright*

by two classes of specialised vessels, a fleet minesweeper to be manned by the Royal Naval Reserve and a single-role minehunter. It is hoped that both classes will keep costs within bounds; a figure of £4½ million a copy for the fleet minesweeper is welcome.

Port and Shipping Organisation

In time of tension and war, the maintenance of shipping traffic in as safe and organised a form as possible is a cardinal need for Britain and, indeed, for the West generally. Many Royal Naval Reserve personnel are trained in Naval Control of Shipping, the organisation which briefs and arranges the movement of merchant ships, forms them into convoys and routes them. Loading, unloading and allocation of cargoes is arranged by the Civil Direction of Shipping in the Department of Transport. Extensive liaison in peacetime with the Merchant Navy and with shipping organisations ensures that procedures are familiar if an emergency should occur. Local support in port administration and defence is provided by the Royal Naval Auxiliary Service. Such voluntary and dedicated organisations form an excellent nucleus for the expansion that would undoubtedly take place in any protracted period of tension.

Below:
Artist's impression of the new single-role minehunter.
Vosper Thornycroft (UK) Ltd

British Non-Fleet Surface Vessels, 1984

Name and Pendant No		Completed	Length feet (metres)	Beam feet (metres)	Speed knots	Displacement tons	Complement
Mine Countermeasures Vessels							
'Ton' Class Minesweepers							
Alfriston	(M1103)						
Bickington	(M1109)						
Crichton	(M1124)						
Crofton	(M1216)						
Cuxton	(M1125)						
Hodgeston	(M1146)	1953-	153	28	16	360	29
Lewiston	(M1208)	1960	(46.6)	(8.5)			
Pollington	(M1173)						
Shavington	(M1180)						
Stubbington	(M1204)						
Upton	(M1187)						
Walkerton	(M1188)						
Wotton	(M1195)						
'Ton' Class Minehunters							
Bildeston	(M1110)						
Bossington	(M1133)						
Brereton	(M1113)						
Brinton	(M1114)						
Bronington	(M1115)						
Gavinton	(M1140)						
Hubberston	(M1147)						
Iveston	(M1151)	1953-	153	28	16	360	38
Kellington	(M1154)	1960	(46.6)	(8.5)			
Kedleston	(M1153)						
Kirkliston	(M1157)						
Maxton	(M1165)						
Nurton	(M1166)						
Sheraton	(M1181)						
Wilton (GRP)	(M1116)						

British Non-Fleet Surface Vessels, 1984 *(cont)*

Name and Pendant No		Completed	Length feet (metres)	Beam feet (metres)	Speed knots	Displacement tons	Complement
'Hunt' Class MCMV							
Brecon	(M29)						
Ledbury	(M30)						
Cattistock	(M31)						
Brocklesby	(M33)						
Dulverton	(M35)	1979-	187	32.8	16	685	40
Cottesmore	(M32)		(57)	(10)			
Middleton *	(M34)						
Chiddingfold *	(M37)						
Hurworth *	(M39)						
Bicester *							
Atherstone *							
'River' Class							
Waveney	(M2003)						
Carron	(M2004)						
Dovey	(M2005)						
Helford *	(M2006)	1984-	154.2	34.4		850	19
Humber *	(M2007)		(47)	(10.5)			
Blackwater *	(M2008)						
Itchen *	(M2009)						
Helmsdale *	(M2010)						
Four planned							
* Building							
'Single Role Minehunter' Class							
Design stage			164	31.2	15		40
			(50)	(9.5)			
Chartered Trawlers							
St David		1972	120.7	29.2	14	392	40
Venturer			(36.6)	(8.9)			
Exercise Minelayer							
Abdiel	(N21)	1967	265	38.5	16	1,370	77
			(80.8)	(11.7)			
Survey Vessels							
Hecla	(A133)	1966					
Hecate	(A137)	1966	260	49	14	2,504	115
Hydra	(A144)	1966	(79.2)	(15)			
Herald	(A138)	1974					
Beagle	(A319)						
Bulldog	(A317)	1968	190	37	15	1,005	39
Fox	(A320)		(57.7)	(11.2)			
Fawn	(A335)						
Echo	(A70)						
Egeria	(A72)	1958-59	106	22	14	140	19
Enterprise	(A71)		(32)	(6.8)			
Gleaner	(A86)	1983	49.2	15.1		20	6
			(15)	(4.6)			

British Non-Fleet Surface Vessels, 1984 *(cont)*

Name and Pendant No		Completed	Length feet (metres)	Beam feet (metres)	Speed knots	Displacement tons	Complement
Offshore Patrol Vessels							
'Bird' Class							
Kingfisher	(P260)						
Cygnet	(P261)	1975-77	120	23	18	190	24
Petrel	(P262)		(36.5)	(7)			
Sandpiper	(P263)						
'Island' Class							
Jersey	(P295)						
Orkney	(P299)						
Shetland	(P298)		195	36	16	1,000	39
Guernsey	(P297)	1976-79	(59.5)	(11)			
Anglesea	(P277)						
Alderney	(P278)						
Lindisfarne	(P300)						
'Castle' Class							
Leeds Castle	(P258)	1979-81	265	37.7	20	1,660	50
Dumbarton Castle	(P265)		(81)	(11.5)			
Hong Kong Patrol Boats							
Peacock	(P239)						
Plover	(P240)		203.4	32.8	24	700	31
Starling	(P241)	1983-	(62)	(10)			
Swallow	(P242)						
Swift	(P243)						
Falkland Islands Patrol Vessels							
Protector	(P244)		194	39		1,000	24
Guardian	(P245)		(58.4)	(11.8)			
Sentinel	(P246)		206	43		1,670	25
			(62.1)	(13.0)			
'Loyal' Class							
Alert	(A510)	1978	80	21	10		12
Vigilant	(A382)		(24.1)	(6.4)			
'20 metre' Class							
Attacker	(P281)						
Fencer	(P283)						
Hunter	(P284)		65.6	17.1		32	11
Striker	(P285)	1983-	(20)	(5.2)			
Chaser	(P282)						
Ice Patrol Ship							
Endurance	(A171)	1968	305	46	15	3,650	124
			(92.9)	(14)			
Seabed Operations Vessel							
Challenger	(K07)	1984	439.6	55.8	15	7,200	173
			(134)	(17)			
Royal Yacht							
Britannia	(A00)	1954	412	55	18	3,900	270
			(125.7)	(16.8)			

8 Fleet Support

To keep a modern, complex, highly technical maritime force at optimum fighting efficiency and readiness, comprehensive stores and maintenance back-up is needed. Even in the days of Pepys it was very difficult to provide logistic support directly from private or commercial sources. It is, therefore, not surprising that nowadays the support organisation is a centrally controlled component of the Ministry of Defence costing, on the Naval side alone, well over a billion pounds a year to run.

Support can be thought of as a flow of material and skills, moving towards a final destination in the Fleet's ships, aircraft and men. It is a largely civilian affair in its earlier stages, and sometimes stays in civilian channels for most of its course. Over 60,000 civilians, indeed, are employed in fleet support; that is, very nearly one for every uniformed member of the Naval service. The flow of support can be divided into two main streams: stores, provisions and fuel; and maintenance, repair and refit.

Stores, Provisions and Fuel

Initial procurement and holding of naval stores (of which there are over 800,000 separate inventory items), armament and victualling stores and fuel, are the responsibility of the Royal Navy Supply and Transport Service (RNSTS) under its civilian director-general, who is responsible in turn to the Chief of Fleet Support, an officer of flag rank who is a member of the Navy Board.

Apart from headquarters staff, the RNSTS has, necessarily, many out-stations. These are not all close to the major naval ports, although of course there are stores departments at all of these, and some stores and most victualling depots are close by. But hardware, armament and fuel depots are quite widely scattered as a consequence of history (that was where they finished World War 2, and new real estate, to say nothing of new buildings and plant, is hard to come by) and policy (dispersal can be helpful in terms both of defence against sabotage, and in bringing employment to places that need it). Nevertheless, under the economic pressures of the last few years there has been a coalescence of facilities. Several depots have been closed, notably at Pembroke Dock (fuel) and Deptford and Woolston (stores). Llangennech, another stores depot, is due to close in 1987.

Computers are extensively used for stock control. Central control of stocking and procurement is carried out at Bath, certain categories of items are subject to functional stock control at depots, and local holdings at naval bases are also under the scrutiny of a computer. These measures have alleviated, though they can never entirely cure, the problem of the vital bit that is not where it is needed; they are also a safeguard against overstocking. In the Royal Naval Armament Depots, too, important advances in test equipment and techniques have been made, driven by the need to provide sophisticated guided missiles and torpedoes to a standard where they need a minimum of shipboard maintenance: where, in fact, they can be treated as 'rounds of ammunition'.

When stores arrive on board ship or shore establishment they are taken on charge by the naval personnel of the Supply Department concerned and issued to users as required. Some computer assistance is used here too, and it can be expected that ships' stores departments will make increasing use of this tool.

In general, ships' main stores and ammunition requirements are supplied when they are in harbour. But with few overseas bases left, it is operationally crippling to rely on harbour supply, as the Falklands conflict showed with such startling clarity. The Navy then reaped the benefit of its facilities, frequently exercised and jealously preserved, for the supply at sea of all kinds of stores, provisions and fuel. The core of these facilities was the Royal Fleet Auxiliary (RFA).

The Royal Fleet Auxiliary

The ships of the RFA, numbering at present 25 hulls with a total gross registered tonnage of over 300,000, occupy an unusual position in international law. They are government ships on non-commercial service, and thus enjoy many of the immunities of a warship; but being non-combatants and civilian-manned, they have many of the freedoms that merchant ships can claim, such as unannounced entry into foreign ports. They fly the blue ensign, and the officers and many of the men regard the RFA as a lifetime career.

In a modern conventionally-powered warship, on-board fuel stocks are consumed in days rather than weeks. Consequently the tanker element of the RFA must be numerous and widely deployed. Tankers are of three kinds: large and small fleet tankers, whose main job is replenishing the fleet at sea, and support tankers which are generally employed in freighting oil supplies in bulk. The fleet tankers are all capable of 19kt or thereabouts and an important operational characteristic of the larger ones is their ability to accommodate up to three Sea

King helicopters from a hangar and flight deck aft. The smaller tankers of the 'Rover' class have a flight deck but no hangar.

Fuelling at sea is a routine operation for both RFAs and warships, but however routine it may be it requires care. Alongside refuelling, the most common technique, requires

Below:
Still the most descriptive photograph of abeam fuelling: RFA *Olna* and HM Ships *London* and *Argonaut* in the early 1970s. The hose on the right is connected, while that on the left is being recovered as *London* breaks away after completing with fuel.
Crown Copyright

Right:
Abeam fuelling is a routine operation, but requires constant care and attention in station-keeping: HMS *Brazen* replenishes in the Mediterranean.
Crown Copyright, photo by Chief Petty Officer Smart

the warship to steam parallel to the tanker at a distance of about 100ft, usually for over an hour. Since the passage of a ship through the water generates zones of pressure at the bow and stern, and of suction amidships, the approach to and disengagement from this close station are times requiring particular alertness. At these same moments the hands on deck are also fully occupied in connecting or disconnecting the gear, doing their best to reduce to a minimum the dead time between the moment when the first line, fired by a line-throwing rifle, goes across and the connection of the hose and the start of pumping by the tanker. The heavy rubber hose is supported by troughs hung from the tanker's derrick or a wire jackstay between the ships. Steady improvements have been made to the gear to improve the speed of coupling and the ability to conduct a clean emergency breakaway. Apart from the hose, only the thin, hand-tended distance indicator line and the telephone communication line connect the two ships.

Another way of fuelling at sea is the astern method. The tanker trails a hose astern, and the receiving ship grapples a line tailed to it and hauls it on board. Once connected, the receiving ship keeps station on the tanker and maintains a bight in the hose as it trails in the water, to minimise strain. The process tends to be more laborious than abeam fuelling, but civilian tankers can be adapted quickly to supply fuel in this way: and laboriously acquired fuel is much better than no fuel at all.

The second large category of RFAs consists of the fleet replenishment ships, which supply armament, victualling and naval stores. They have complements drawn from both the RFA and RNSTS, since of course stores holding and issue is much more complex than that of fuel. As well as computerised stock control, there is extensive use of palletised loads, powered roller transporters and closed circuit television to control cargo flow.

Above:
Vertical replenishment of relatively light and urgent stores is done by helicopter. *Crown Copyright*

Below:
Transferring personnel by light jackstay. *Crown Copyright*

The Royal Fleet Auxiliary, 1984

Name and Pendant No		Completed	Length feet (metres)	Beam feet (metres)	Speed knots	Displacement tons	Complement
Fleet tankers							
Olwen	(A122)	1965					
Olmeda	(A124)	1965	648 (197.5)	84 (25.6)	19	19,200	94
Olna	(A123)	1967					
Tidespring	(A75)	1963	582.7 (177.6)	70.9 (21.6)	18	14,450	110
Green Rover	(A268)						
Grey Rover	(A269)						
Blue Rover	(A270)	1969-74	461 (140.5)	62.3 (19)	19	7,700	48
Gold Rover	(A271)						
Black Rover	(A273)						
Freighting tankers							
Brambleleaf	(A81)	1980					
Appleleaf	(A79)	1979	561 (171)	85.3 (26)	16	21,090	65
Bayleaf	(A109)	1982					
Pearleaf	(A77)	1960	567.6 (173)	72.2 (22)	16	12,900	55
Plumleaf	(A78)	1960	561 (171)	72.2 (22)	16	13,060	55
Fleet Replenishment Ships							
Resource	(A480)	1967	640 (195)	77 (23.5)	21	18,580	123
Regent	(A486)						
Fort Grange	(A385)	1978	603.7 (184)	78.7 (24)	22	16,520	133
Fort Austin	(A386)	1979					
Logistic Landing Ships							
Sir Lancelot	(L3029)						
Sir Geraint	(L3027)						
Sir Bedivere	(L3004)	1964-68	410.4 (125.1)	64.4 (19.6)	17	4,620	65
Sir Percivale	(L3036)						
Sir Tristram	(L3505)						
Sir Caradoc	(L3522)	1983	406.8 (124)	52.5 (16)	17	3,560	26
Sir Lamorak	(L3532)	1983	355.3 (108.3)	66.9 (20.4)	17	2,725	20
Helicopter Support Ship							
Engadine	(K08)	1967	423.2 (129)	58.1 (17.7)	14	6,710	73+ RN personnel
Argus							
ARAPAHO Ship							
Reliant		Charter 1983	669.2 (204)	101 (30.8)		23,370	211

Solids replenishment at sea generates a ship-handling and station-keeping problem similar to that of fuelling, except that the heavy jackstay gear used demands that distances apart are even smaller. The wire jackstay, hauled across and secured to a strong point in the receiving ship, is kept taut by a self-tensioning winch in the RFA and forms a high-wire across which a traveller carrying the stores can be hauled back and forth. One of the most difficult problems in the receiving ship is moving the stores quickly away from the reception point without denting the deck, the upperworks, the stores themselves, or the sailors moving them.

The next generation of replenishment ships of the RFA will embody a different concept: that of the 'one-stop ship', a vessel carrying all kinds of stores and capable of supplying ammunition, solid stores and fuel in a single replenishment operation. These Auxiliary Oilers Replenishment (AORs), which will come into service in the 1990s, will also have facilities not only to operate several Sea King and EH 101 helicopters but to provide second-line maintenance for them. This will greatly help the frigates, particularly the Type 23s, that operate such aircraft. In fact the flexibility of large-helicopter operations, in both the vertical replenishment and ASW roles, will be much enhanced by the AOR concept.

Training for helicopter crews in basic shipboard operating is another function the RFA can fulfil. RFA *Engadine* at present carries out this job for the Sea Training organisation at Portland; she will eventually be relieved by the much larger and better equipped RFA *Argus* (ex-*Contender Bezant*, a Falklands veteran) which could also have a significant wartime role as a helicopter ship and mobile spare deck.

Some mention must be made of the logistic landing ships which operated with such gallantry in the South Atlantic. The names *Sir Galahad* and *Sir Tristram* will be enough to remind readers what risks they ran. Five – including the refitted *Sir Tristram* – survive; with the replacement *Sir Galahad*, and a new pair, *Sir Lamorak* and *Sir Caradoc*, they will continue to be manned by the RFA and run mainly on behalf of the Army. By their flexibility and adaptability to many kinds of amphibious operation they have shown what important units they are.

Maintenance, Repair and Refit
Like any other pieces of machinery, ships, aircraft and submarines cannot run without servicing and maintenance. Into the programme of every vessel are planned periods alongside with help from the Fleet Maintenance Units, teams of Naval personnel who augment the ship's company in order to complete planned maintenance work and put right defects that affect the ship's fighting efficiency. Such periods generally occur in the home ports, but teams can be flown to places abroad with the host country's agreement.

Naturally these assisted maintenance periods make use of the shore facilities that are available, but their emphasis is on putting things right 'in place', not taking them to pieces and carting them away to be refurbished. However, there comes a time in the life of any unit when it is necessary to do deeper and heavier work of that kind; and this is the fundamental purpose of the Royal Dockyards. As this book is written, the number of dockyards with a full range of facilities for refit and repair, with a large skilled civilian workforce, will reduce to two: only Devonport and Rosyth will remain, Chatham will close completely and Portsmouth will join Faslane and Portland as a naval base which has numerous material support facilities and considerable skilled civilian manpower but does not offer the capacity to rebuild a ship more or less from the keel up.

Below:
A busy deck during replenishment of solid stores.
Crown Copyright

FORT GRANGE

A385

Ships of the Royal Fleet Auxiliary

Above:
RFA Fort Grange, Fleet Replenishment Ship.

Left:
RFA Brambleleaf, support tanker.

Below left:
RFA Sir Lamorak, logistic landing ship. *All Crown Copyright*

Below:
Artist's impression of the AOR, to be brought into service within the decade and to carry a mixture of stores, ammunition and fuel. *Crown Copyright*

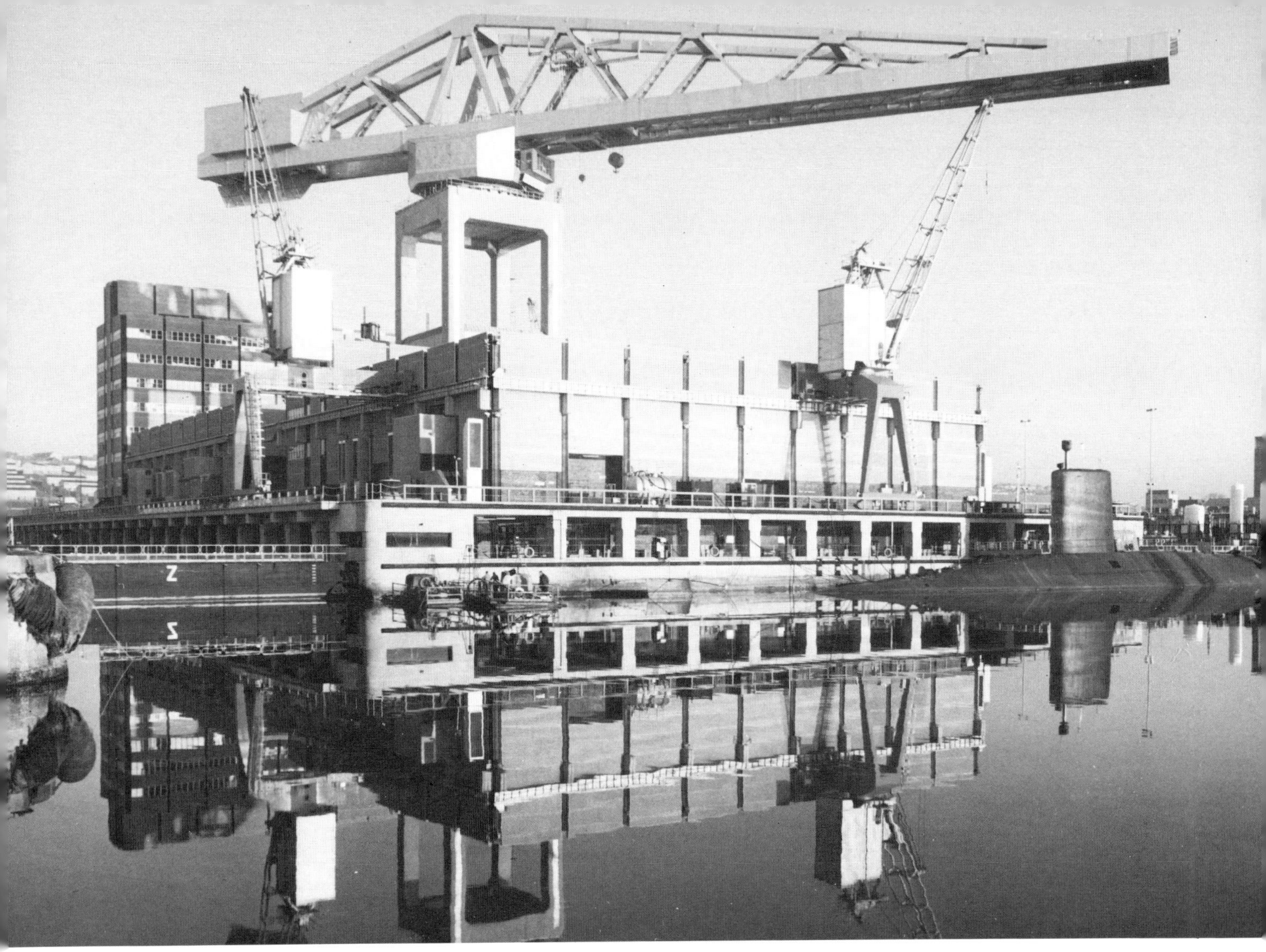

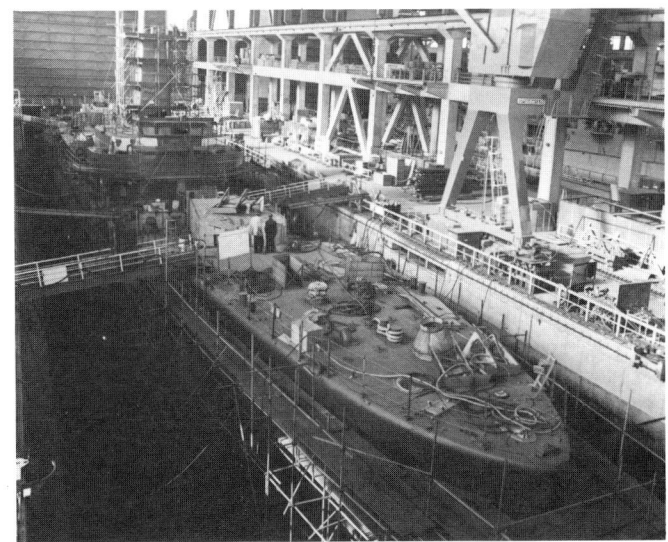

It was perhaps too enthusiastic a pursuit of that ability that led to the present closures. The refit and particularly the mid-life modernisation of warships were, as has been shown, singularly ambitious in the case of the 'Leander' class, and there is no doubt that the expense of time and money to produce one Batch 3 conversion – Sea Wolf-armed and packed with ASW sophistication though it might be – scared accounting officers and ministers silly. Whether the remedy was not too harsh, as many have argued, time will tell. It is not easy to envisage how a force of 17 fleet and four ballistic missile submarines is to be sustained by only two nuclear refitting facilities (the third was at Chatham); nor how a force of even 50 destroyers/frigates, up to five heavy ships, and the RFA, surveying and mine countermeasures forces can be refitted, even without comprehensive modernisation, in the Royal yards alone; nor how battle damage may be expeditiously repaired with the facilities that remain. Perhaps it is planned to give more work out to civilian yards, as happened in the case of the refits of HM ships *Euryalus* and *Otter* in 1984; or perhaps that will happen even if it is not planned.

Like all other aspects of this vexed and emotionally-charged problem, that last point turns on the question of efficiency. Ship repair and refit is a highly complex operation, demanding exceptional diagnostic skill, imaginative planning and flexible working practices in a highly proficient workforce. There have been times when the dockyards lived up to those almost utopian standards, the last of them being the hectic days before the Falklands Task Force put to sea and dockyard mateys 'with

Above:
The nuclear submarine refitting facility at Devonport, now being extended as a result of the closure of Chatham Dockyard.
Crown Copyright

Below:
In the covered frigate complex at Devonport. *Crown Copyright*

Right:
The RMAS mooring, salvage and boom vessel *Goosander*, which saw service in the Falklands in 1982. *Crown Copyright*

redundancy notices in their pockets' performed miracles of ingenuity. But all too often, in routine circumstances, ships' completion dates have fallen behind and work has taken far more time and effort than it should. Like much of British industry, the dockyards have been a high-skill, low-wage, low-productivity, rule-bound organisation. It would have taken quite inspired management and leadership to make sense of such a contradictory set of criteria, and as in British industry elsewhere under the same conditions – including the civilian shipyards – such management has been only rarely available.

It is important not to blink these unpleasant sights, for keeping fighting units in trim is a very important aspect of sea power and indeed of deterrence. Many changes, more or less radical, have been suggested over the years. The latest, called the Levine proposals after the Chairman of the Committee which suggested them, entail retention of the Dockyards' assets in public hands but management by a private contractor: the 'agency management model'. At the time of writing these proposals remain in the balance.

To turn to the repair of aircraft, the Royal Navy in fact runs the helicopter repair organisation for all three fighting services. This is based at the Royal Naval Aircraft Yards at Fleetlands and Wroughton. The total number of rotary-wing aircraft supported is nearly 900, and of these up to 200 pass through the RNAYs each year. Engine overhauls total more than 300 a year; these are done at Fleetlands only. Perhaps because they are a compound of younger crafts and skills and have to deal with fewer of the residues of industrial history, the RNAYs enjoy an enviable reputation for efficiency.

The Royal Maritime Auxiliary Service

A large number of harbour craft, civilian-manned, provide services to the Fleet in the home ports. There are lighters and launches, mooring craft, waterboats, fuel carriers, trials vessels and about 50 tugs. They too, however humbly, are a part of sea power.

The National Infrastructure

Finally in this chapter it is necessary to mention all too briefly that large body of assets that is not in peacetime under government control but can be taken up in time of tension or war. The South Atlantic campaign was an eye-opener to all but a very few in this respect. Contingency plans did exist to take up ships from trade but their extent was not generally known; the final tally showed 45 merchant vessels and five trawlers used in this way. Some were fitted with flight decks, all with fuelling-at-sea arrangements and communication and cryptographic equipment. Their officers and crews, all volunteers, rose magnificently to the occasion as British merchant seamen always have.

Other aspects of the civil end of British sea power were used, even if not so overtly. The Falklands White Paper mentions 'civilian ports . . . together with hundreds of industrial firms large and small', and it is clear that as so often before, the advantages of a maritime heritage and a healthy use of the sea in peacetime at once became apparent in war. Mahan made the point; it is necessary only to reiterate it.

But, in these days when wholly natural economic growths are rare, the maritime infrastructure is likely to need support at certain points. Today it may look like the civilian shipyards; tomorrow, the offshore oil industry; the day after, the dry-cargo merchant fleet; the day after that, all three. Governments will not find it easy to choose their beneficiaries, even if they are in the mood to donate goodies. But, for the prudent government in a medium maritime power, it will be proper at least to attempt as accurate an analysis as possible of the health and strength of the maritime base. There is not much evidence that any such analysis is in progress in Britain.

9 The Women's Royal Naval Service

Whether, in an age that is sensitive about discrimination in any sense, it is wise to include a separate chapter on the WRNS is not clear. But it seems on balance better to do so than not, because its inclusion only in a chapter on 'personnel', or some similarly bland word, would give a less than fair indication of the contribution to British sea power made by this separate yet increasingly integrated, nautically-dedicated yet land-bound service.

Founded in 1917 with the simple slogan 'Free a man to fight', the WRNS overcame interwar disbandment to reach a peak strength of 74,600 in 1945. Its distinguished service in World War 2 unassailably secured its position in the postwar naval service, though of course numbers rapidly dropped to under a tenth of the wartime strength.

A series of far-reaching organisational reforms was introduced in the mid-1970s. Wrens came under the Naval Discipline Act, their appointing and drafting was conducted by the same organisations that managed the rest of the service, and officers' training was moved from Greenwich to Dartmouth. All these changes made it possible to align the background of WRNS and RN personnel more closely, and increase their interchangeability for many tasks ashore. It also meant that the smaller service needed fewer of its own people to carry out its administration, since so many of the procedures were now common and no special expertise was required.

The whole movement, in fact, was towards integration of the WRNS and RN, but this was not carried to its limits. First, it has always been a tenet of WRNS philosophy that its personnel are not a fighting force. Their skills much improve the fighting efficiency of the Fleet but they are not trained as weapon handlers or controllers. Second, Wrens are never posted to seagoing ships and only occasionally do day-work at sea. Many of the specialisations acquired by male ratings are, therefore, inappropriate and Wrens are not trained in these. Finally, there remain some elements of uniform – notably blue stripes and badges – that are a symbol of these continuing differences.

Officer Structure

WRNS officers are drawn in about equal proportions from three sources: graduates, often selected during their final year at University; civilians with two 'A' levels, who enter as cadets; and WRNS ratings who have achieved five GCE 'O' level passes. All have to satisfy the Admiralty Interview Board that they have the potential to become officers, and all who enter from civilian life spend some time as ratings at the initial training establishment and elsewhere; in the case of the graduates this is short, but enough to give them a necessary idea of the pattern of WRNS life.

Careers thereafter follow a wide variety of patterns. Supply and Secretariat officers are very largely interchangeable, ashore, with their male counterparts. Not only can they act as secretaries to senior officers but can also take on catering and mess management, pay and cash charge and accounting. Communications officers again undergo a largely common training; work in shore headquarters and operational establishments and schools occupies them very largely. WRNS operations officers are a relatively new breed, certainly somewhat differently trained from the warfare officers who are their nearest counterparts at sea but sharing a common skill in the growing field of automatic data processing. The Air side of the service sees a good deal of WRNS officers, including those in the meteorological and air traffic control specialisations. Finally, a number of WRNS officers specialise in careers and personnel selection work, and a few more in public relations.

Rating Structure

WRNS ratings are drawn from the 17-28 age group. The educational qualifications required vary quite widely according to the branch for which the candidate is being considered. A few require 'A' levels, the majority much less. At the time of

Below:
A World War 1 Wren Air Mechanic. *Crown Copyright*

Above:
Three generations on: a Wren Air Engineering Mechanic (Weapons Electrical) working on an aircraft. *Crown Copyright*

Left:
Wrens (Radar) working in a training simulator at the School of Maritime Operations, HMS *Dryad*. *Crown Copyright*

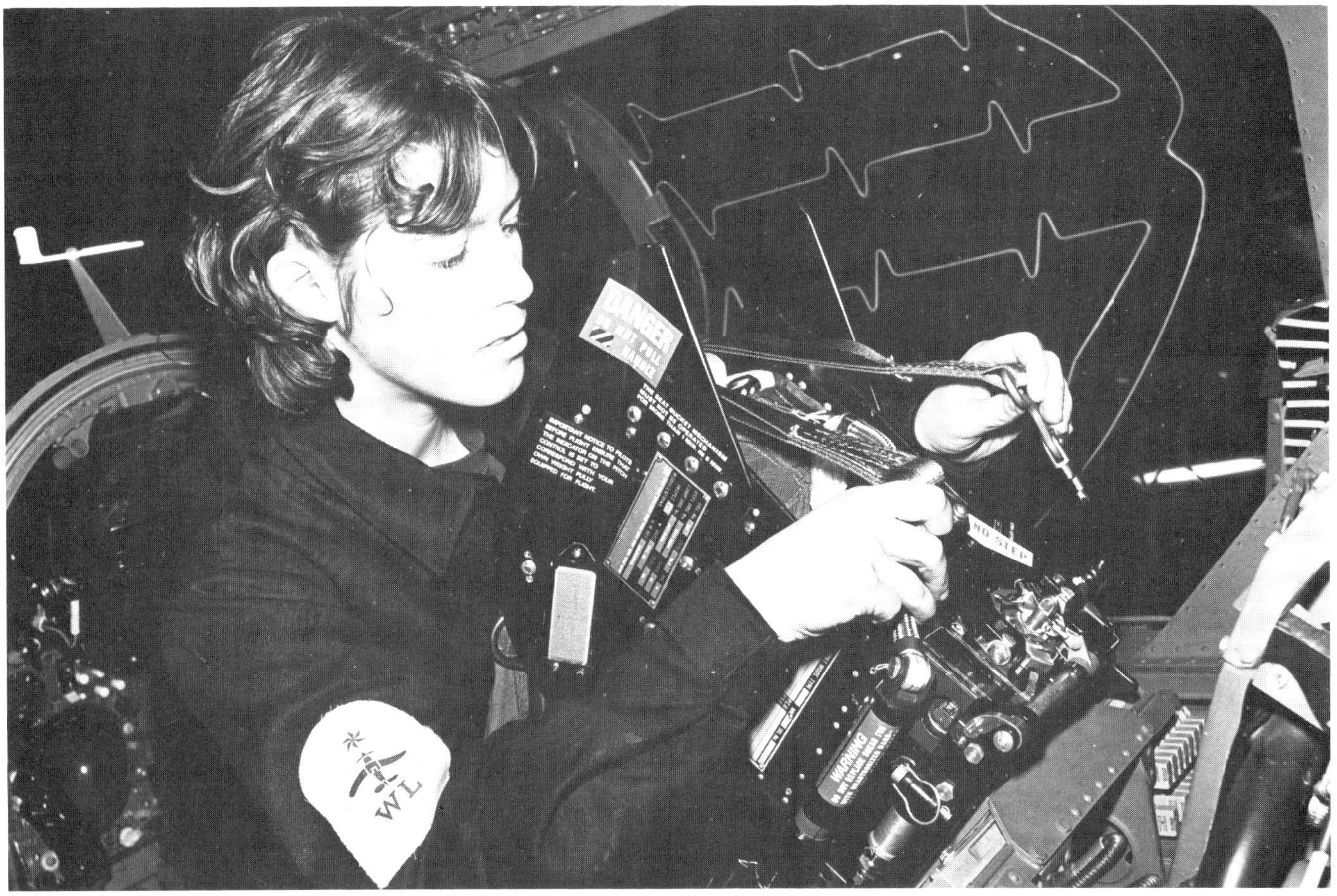

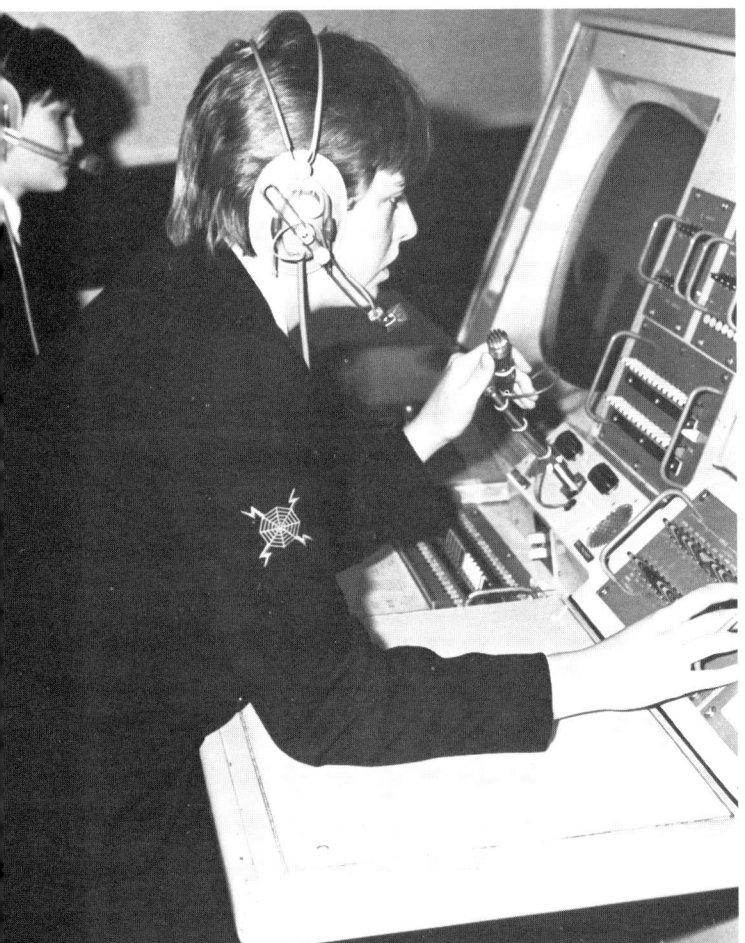

writing there were, as with the officer entry, many more candidates than places available.

On joining for new entry training at HMS *Raleigh*, near Torpoint in Cornwall, a rating has 14 days' probation at the end of which she may leave if she, or the service, decide that life in the WRNS is not for her. If she decides to enrol it will be for a nine-year period initially, though engagements can be terminated at 18 months' notice at any time and at four months' notice in order to marry.

As for the officers, specialist training is aligned with that for the RN whenever appropriate. In the Supply and Secretariat specialisation, categories include writers who sub-specialise in either pay and accounting or general secretarial work; stores accountants who have custody and control (often computerised) of all manner of supplies; stewards who work in officers' messes; and cooks who may work in officers', ships' companies' or general galleys. The operations branch consists of radar ratings, working mainly in shore simulators with a variety of display and data processing equipment; and radio operators, who are fully interchangeable with RN ratings in shore billets. Meteorological observers, photographers and physical training instructors, too, fill most complement billets ashore regardless of sex. Air engineering mechanics are

trained to a high level of skill, with an outlet to the higher rates in the mechanician scheme.

Some categories are exclusive to the WRNS. They include education assistants, who administer education centres and do some teaching, training support assistants, who are specialists in visual and audio training aids, telephonists, dental surgery assistants and hygienists, and motor transport drivers. Some WRNS ratings are specialised in family service work, others in the administration of WRNS quarters. Finally, the popular

Left:
A Chief Wren Writer (Pay) paying ratings' cash claims.
Crown Copyright

Below:
A First Officer WRNS Public Relations Officer giving information to the Press after a search and rescue incident.
Crown Copyright

weapons analyst category is employed assessing the results of all kinds of Fleet weapon practices, a task of great interest and evident importance.

In an Establishment

In a shore establishment, WRNS living quarters are separate, generally modern and always well furnished. Messing and social life is normally integrated with that of the establishment. The part that Wrens can take at work is clear, but their role in the wider aspects of establishment life is in many ways just as important. In social activities – based on the ratings' clubs and officers' messes – and in all forms of recreation from the annual Drama Festival to sailing and gliding events, they are invariably cheerful and active participants. It is hard to find anyone in the Navy who does not regard them as an enriching and civilising influence, particularly so in the remoter establishments.

Promotion ladders are, in such a small service, very much dependent on the individuals concerned, particularly in the smaller categories. Advancement for ratings may not be particularly quick, and for officers the achievement of a permanent commission – initial engagements are all for a limited career – is an important hurdle. However, the rate of natural wastage in the WRNS is rather higher than in the male service and this tends to even matters up. Many girls do, of course, leave the service on marriage; but those who wish to remain after marriage may do so, if they are prepared to serve wherever required. In those cases where both partners are in the service, every effort is made to draft them to the same establishment or area, particularly when the husband is due for some time ashore.

The WRNS as an Element of Sea Power

Each woman in the WRNS does her job as well as she may, and that may often be better than most or all men could. That is one good reason for the WRNS. On the other hand, because Wrens are not trained to combatant tasks (and even Israel now keeps women out of the front line, so the UK is in general company) and therefore cannot help to man warships, they do induce an element of inflexibility into the system. That might be thought a reason for abolishing the WRNS. But in fact, because it is necessary to keep operational the absolute maximum of our depleted fleet, the sea to shore ratio of male ratings must be higher than in the past; thus, the availability of Wrens to man shore billets is a positive advantage. Moreover, this applies particularly to the junior rates (where a high proportion of Wrens are found) because male junior rates now do most of their training at sea.

All in all, therefore, the Wrens are, if not day by day 'freeing a man to fight', at least freeing a substantial proportion of the male Navy to get to sea and keep the fleet manned. At the same time they are carrying out their own tasks with cheerfulness and efficiency and enhancing sea power directly. Finally, they act as a nucleus for a much larger service that might be required if tension increased or large-scale conflict occurred. They are not an investment that should be foregone.

10 Organisation and Training

When, nearly two decades ago now, a group of senior officers were discussing a major reorganisation of the Royal Navy's command structure, they became involved in problems of definition. What, exactly, did 'organisation' mean? Worse, what did 'administration' mean? They concluded that administration was what organisation did most of the time, and that organisation was something that did administration.

The writer cannot do better, but can try to put it another way. To use the dangerous analogy of the human body, organisation can be likened to the brain and central nervous system, administration to the direction of that system for the maintenance of the body in good condition; to extend the analogy a trifle, training is the familiarisation of every member of the body in the functions it is expected to conduct, and operational command and control is the direction, through the nervous system, of the conduct of those functions.

The analogy is not, of course, a precise one, and this is nowhere more apparent than in the higher reaches of the provision and exercise of sea power, where not only are there many tiers of decision-making but the decisions concerned are of very different kinds. As civil servants are fond of saying, the Ministry of Defence is a department of state not a headquarters, and this makes it qualitatively different from the office of a commander-in-chief as well as occupying a superior place in the hierarchy.

The Ministry of Defence
Precisely where power lies in the Ministry of Defence is a subject on which one could write a book – and still be correct only for a given set of personalities. There is no question that ultimate power lies with the Secretary of State and his ministers. It is they who have the final say, before Cabinet and

Parliament, in both strategy and allocation of money: the two really critical areas of long-term decision-making. But below ministerial level it is not simply a matter of carrying out instructions, nor of making cases to persuade ministers; there are all sorts of subsidiary decisions to be made that affect not only present projects and operations but future policies. The machinery for taking such decisions has recently been changed quite considerably by ministerial decision. Broadly, the change has been in the direction of reducing the autonomy of the single services in policy and decision making, and concentrating power in a central defence staff under the Chief of Defence Staff, with an input – equally if not more powerful – from the civilian Permanent Under Secretary. This will be most noticeable probably in the programmes for procurement of new systems and, consequently, in the direction in which the structures of all the services will move. The Admiralty Board (which may be renamed the Navy Board) will be considered a management, rather than a policy-making, body. The First Sea Lord, advised by a smaller but still substantial staff, will remain professional head of the service. Personnel organisation and training, and fleet support, will remain functions of the Navy Board. But it appears that much of the necessary co-ordination of effort with scientific staffs, establishments and firms in the procurement of equipment will, at least nominally, become a function of the central staff.

Thus a great deal of the policy and provision of British sea power comes down from the Ministry of Defence. Detailed management of the Royal Navy comes under two commanders-in-chief: C-in-C Fleet, with his headquarters in Northwood, and C-in-C Naval Home Command, at Portsmouth.

C-in-C Fleet

The Commander-in-Chief Fleet has under command all the operational ships and submarines, and embarked aircraft, of the Royal Navy. His headquarters near London is convenient for the essential co-operation with the Royal Air Force – the commander of the long-range maritime reconnaissance element is co-located at Northwood and the AOC-in-C Strike Command close by at High Wycombe – and for communication with the Ministry of Defence, and not inconvenient for visiting the ships of the fleet, which he frequently does. The Flag Officer Submarines is also at Northwood. The system was comprehensively tested in 1982 and came through well.

Surface ships are divided into three flotillas, each under the command of a flag officer. These are the officers who can be expected to take charge of group deployments in either peace or war; Rear Adm 'Sandy' Woodward was FOF1 when he sailed for the South Atlantic. Under the Flag Officers there is further subdivision into squadrons each under a captain, so that for example all Ikara 'Leanders' are at present under the command of the Captain, First Frigate Squadron. All these

senior officers are supported by appropriate staffs so that material and personnel can be satisfactorily administered.

C-in-C Naval Home Command

The Commander-in-Chief Naval Home Command has under command all naval shore establishments, except naval air stations, in the United Kingdom and has overall responsibility for co-ordinating the implementation of training policy as laid down by the Board. These responsibilities give him about the same number of active servicemen under command as the C-in-C Fleet. He also has responsibility for the Reserves, a force which, as regular naval forces become ever more stretched, will increase in importance.

The flag officers at Portsmouth and Plymouth are also Port Admirals, with overall responsibility for administering the port for support of the fleet. At Rosyth the Flag Officer Scotland & Northern Ireland has an unusually heavy operational task, conducting as he does – in co-ordination with the Royal Air Force – fishery and oil rig protection and surveillance of Soviet naval activity.

NATO Aspects

Nearly every commander so far mentioned has a corresponding NATO function which he carries out in exercises, tension or war and for which he may sometimes have a permanent

Above:
Sport is part of the Dartmouth curriculum . . .

Above right:
. . . Rigorous training too. *Crown Copyright, photos by Mr C. Risk*

multi-national staff. Thus C-in-C Fleet is also the Commander-in-Chief Eastern Atlantic Area (CINCEAST-LANT) and Allied Commander-in-Chief Channel (CIN-CHAN); Flag Officer Plymouth is Commander Central Atlantic Area under CINCEASTLANT and is also the Commander of the Plymouth sub-area of the Channel Command. The Air Officer Commanding No 18 Group, RAF, is also Commander of Maritime Air Forces Eastern Atlantic.

Training

But if the end-product is to be a maritime service that is ready at all times to carry out any operational task laid upon it, and thereby to deter aggression, the path to that readiness must lie in a carefully thought out and thoroughly implemented training programme both ashore and afloat. The rest of this chapter covers, all too briefly, some aspects of the training pattern. It will, perforce, be very largely about the Navy; but the corresponding and no less intense training in the maritime side of the RAF must not be forgotten, as an important contribution to sea power.

Officers

In any ship's wardroom enquiry will quickly show that the officers have reached their current rank by several different routes. This one may have decided to join the service while at University; another may have had no other ambition since he was 10, got a reserved place at the age of 16 and gone to Dartmouth after passing his 'A' levels; another may have joined as a rating with good educational qualifications, have been selected early as an officer and now be in the main career stream; a fourth may have become a petty officer at 25 and then decided to acquire the necessary qualifications and recommendation for the Special Duties List.

The ways are diverse and even bewildering, and the right place for a detailed description is the recruiting literature and

not this book. It should be added, though, that all aspiring officers except doctors and dentists have to pass the Admiralty Interview Board, which uses its fund of experience to judge whether a candidate's character, abilities and potential measure up to the service; and will do some time at the Britannia Royal Naval College, Dartmouth and under training in the fleet, to acquire basic sea knowledge, skills and leadership.

All officers qualify either as seaman, engineer, supply and secretariat or instructor specialists, and throughout their careers – but particularly in the early years – can expect substantial further training to fit them for their specialisations. The majority of seamen, for example, will qualify as Principal Warfare Officers, expert in the work of an operations room when the ship is in action; supply officers will do a Supply Charge course to enable them to take charge of the supply department of a ship. Instructor officers generally join as graduates and spend much of their time teaching but can expect some sea time, particularly in the meteorological sub-specialisation.

The Engineers undergo a particularly rigorous academic training. The Royal Naval Engineering College at Manadon is in all but name a technical university; degrees are awarded through the Council for National Academic Awards, and the degree and application courses, backed by instructors and facilities that are unrivalled in their field, lead to fully chartered status. A number of seaman officers, as well as all the engineer specialists, now do the Manadon course, an augury perhaps for increasing cross-training and cross-appointing particularly between the seaman and weapons electrical officer.

Flying as a specialisation continues to absorb a large proportion of officers, and many of these will opt for a relatively short initial commission of eight years. In this sort of commission passage through Dartmouth is fairly brisk and there is no fleet time: the officer will wish, and the Navy will wish him, to start flying as a pilot or observer (what a misnomer the latter title is! 'Tactical Director' would be a better description) as soon as possible.

Ratings

The alternative methods of entry for ratings are scarcely less varied than those for officers, and their subsequent paths are even more diverse. The most usual way of joining is as a junior

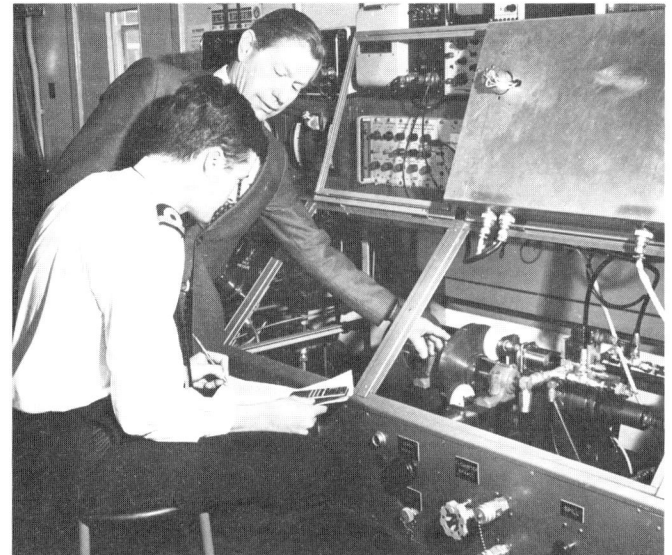

from 16 to 17½ years of age, though adult entries from 17½ to 33 are equally acceptable. Recruiting tests, mental and physical, are simple but not slack; the Navy has learnt to its cost that setting too low a standard results only in high drop-out rates and much disappointment and waste.

Initial training for entrants is at HMS *Raleigh*, where a short sharp five-week course accustoms the young sailor to service discipline and standards as well as teaching basic skills. Those who wish to stay on in the Navy – there is an option of leaving in the first few months – go on to specialist training, at first at other shore establishments and then at sea, in the operations, engineering, supply and secretariat or air branches. The number of sub-specialisations runs into dozens: examples are radar, mine warfare, radio operator (tactical), cook, weapon engineering mechanic and stores accountant. The need to keep as many ships operational as possible will mean, for most of the 1980s and probably beyond, a high sea-to-shore ratio for each man's service, and he will be more likely than in the past to spend most of his career in one type of ship, so that expensive and time-consuming retraining in different systems is avoided. Because ships of the same type will have the same base port, a rating's family is likely to have a more settled domestic environment, which is a 'plus' for the new system. The steps through which a rating can expect to advance, as he acquires the necessary experience, qualifications and recommendations, are leading hand, petty officer, chief petty officer and the ultimate and highly responsible rate of fleet chief petty officer, a full equivalent to warrant rank in the other services. At any stage up to the age of 34, provided he has the sometimes stringent educational qualifications and is considered fully fitted in all other ways, he can be selected to become an officer. Some 25% of all officers in the Royal Navy began their careers on the lower deck.

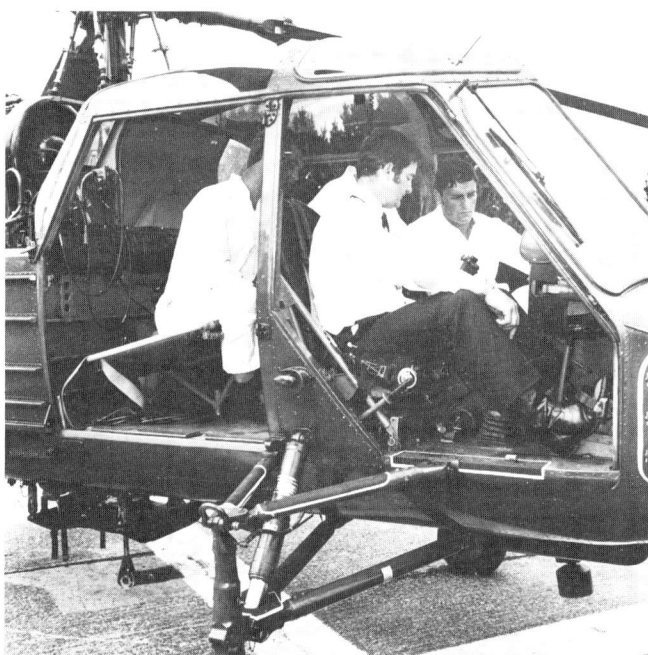

Left:
General and vocational training at the Royal Naval Engineering College, Manadon. *Crown Copyright*

Below:
A general view of the Royal Naval Engineering College. *Crown Copyright*

Left:
Training at HMS *Raleigh*. Boatwork on the river; and heavier seamanship on a simulated rig ashore. *Crown Copyright*

Below left:
Vocational training for naval stewards. *Crown Copyright*

Of these, of course, quite a number began as artificers, a rate not yet mentioned. These are young men of good (that is to say several 'O' levels) educational qualification who do a naval apprenticeship in one of nine specialisations in maintenance and repair skills. They advance quickly to chief petty officer rate after a certain amount of sea time. The added operational flexibility given to a ship by its artificer rates is incalculable. Their technical initiative and inventiveness, springing from their deep knowledge and skill, has kept many a ship going and able to fight when it would otherwise have had to 'fall out of the line'.

The Medical Services

Doctors and dentists enter the Royal Navy after qualifying as such, though some may have been awarded cadetships and thus helped financially. While the Royal Navy operates two hospitals at Haslar, near Portsmouth, and Stonehouse at Plymouth, and sick quarters at other bases, medical and dental officers can expect to spend some of their time afloat. For example, each Polaris crew has a doctor and all large ships have dental as well as medical staffs.

Above:
Medical services require particular training for sea conditions. *Crown Copyright*

Below:
A QARNNS Leading State Registered Nurse assisted by a State Enrolled Nurse prepares the pre-medication of a patient before his operation. *Crown Copyright*

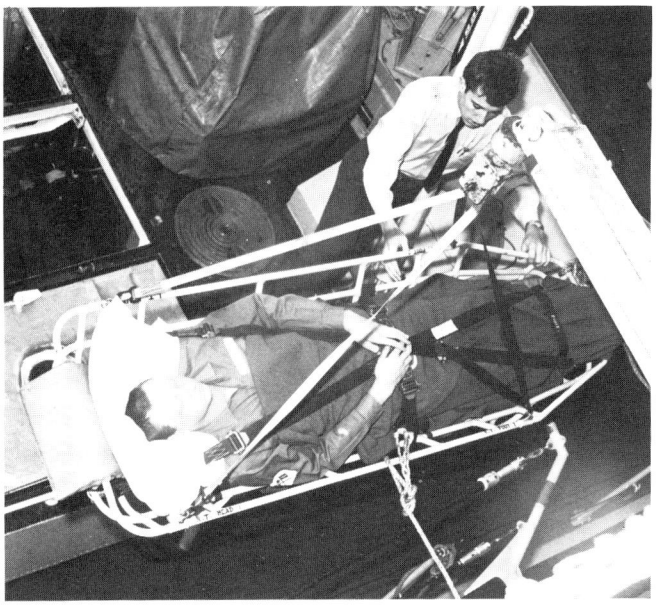

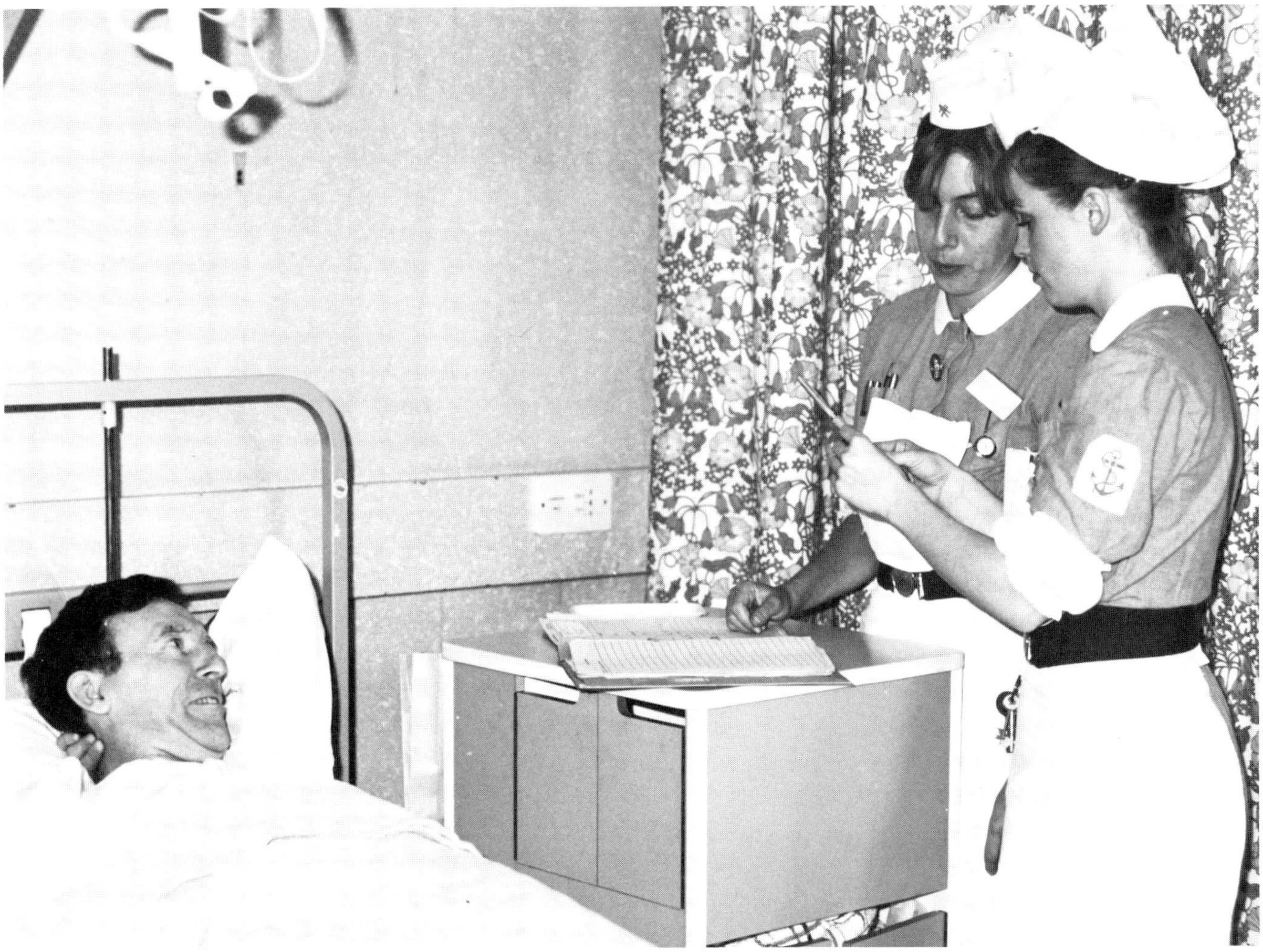

Top:
HMS *Hydra*, a surveying ship converted for ambulance work in the Falklands. *Crown Copyright*

Above:
Medical care for friend and foe alike in the Falklands campaign. *Crown Copyright*

Medical ratings fall into two categories: assistants, whose general training enables them to become the only medically trained person in many small ships, and technicians, who may include those with state registered nurse (SRN) qualifications in highly skilled fields such as radiography and physiotherapy.

Finally, Queen Alexandra's Royal Naval Nursing Service (QARNNS), now open to both men and women, completes the naval medical service. They do not normally serve at sea, but are represented in over a score of shore establishments including, of course, the two main naval hospitals. Nursing officers must have the SRN qualification.

The medical services were severely tested in the Falklands conflict. In SS *Uganda*, in the ambulance ships hastily adapted from the surveying fleet, and ashore at Ajax Bay, they performed prodigious feats. All parts of the service, including

QARNNS, were there. Their proud claim was that of all casualties treated, British and Argentinian (and medical need was the only priority), over 90% survived. They seemed to get pretty short commons when the medals were distributed; perhaps that was because they all deserved one.

Chaplains
In the Royal Navy a chaplain has no rank other than chaplain and that of his office in the church, with all the approachability that that status brings. Anyone who has served in the Royal Navy will know the influence on the life of a naval community that a chaplain can exert; this has not slackened in modern times. Chaplains of all denominations serve ashore and afloat, and with Royal Marine Commando forces.

The Reserves
The Royal Fleet Reserve consists of men and women who have recently left the regular service and can therefore be considered fully trained as well as, by their terms of service, available to be recalled in emergency. The Royal Naval Reserve, some 5,000 strong at present, consists of volunteers who give up one evening a week, and a fortnight each year, to be trained in operational tasks such as mine countermeasures, offshore operations, naval control of shipping and manning shore headquarters. It includes, in List 1, many Merchant Navy officers who bring to it their own particular professionalism and expertise. A high proportion of the captains of Falklands STUFT were in fact RNR officers, though they kept their merchant navy 'hats' for the operation. Finally, the 2,500 members of the Royal Naval Auxiliary Service are trained to provide local support in the area of their homes in time of need; typically they would help to man port headquarters and run naval port organisations. The existence of all the Reserve organisations is a vital contribution to maritime readiness and a nucleus for expansion in a time of protracted tension or conflict.

The Sharp End of Training
Even with an increase in 'typecasting' throughout his career, a man will need to be brought up to date, particularly after a

spell ashore, with the characteristics of his next ship. This can be done in shore establishments by means of simulators during a period of pre-joining training. As an example, the School of Maritime Operations, HMS *Dryad*, provides operations rooms modelled precisely on certain classes of ship and operating, so far as digital ingenuity can devise, in the same way, so that ships' teams can work up their procedures and skills in the business of collecting information, assessing tactical situations and controlling forces and weapons to deal with them.

But the sea waits at the end of the road, and is a tougher environment than the most complex simulator. It is the Royal Navy's policy, therefore, to put all ships through the sea training organisation at Portland, under the eye of the Flag Officer Sea Training and his dedicated staff of 'Sea Riders'. The summary following describes one ship's week of 'Continuation Operational Sea Training' (COST). There are similar weeks stretching either side of this one, up to six in all. It was tempering processes such as these that helped to forge the resilient and resourceful skill and spirit that won in the South Atlantic.

There are many exercises and training periods more complex than Portland, though none so intense for the whole of a ship's company. NATO of course conducts some exercises of great scale, and so does the Fleet nationally, almost always in co-operation with the RAF. Special joint RN/RAF exercises are held under the aegis of the Joint Maritime Operations Training School (JMOTS) in Scotland. Group deployments, as they go round the world, do so in highly operational modes. Maritime forces cannot afford to rest on their laurels, nor do they.

Left:
A Royal Naval Auxiliary Service vessel and its commander, Mrs Denise St Aubyn Hubbard. *Crown Copyright*

Below:
On the sweep deck of a Royal Naval Reserve minesweeper. *Crown Copyright*

One Ship's Week in Work-Up

Monday Leave harbour at 9am (that won't happen again this week). Three ships are in company; the junior one is co-ordinating the departure today. After clearing harbour, line manoeuvres are conducted: good practice for the officer of the watch, helmsman and engine room, nail-biting for the captain. At 9.30 the missile system is exercised by mock aircraft attacks, and at 10 jamming aircraft join in. At 11.45 the air is buzzing with helicopters as sea-riding staff are winched on and off the ships in preparation for the afternoon serials. Come noon, some people get lunch, but others are exercising the seaboat and the ship's rescue swimmers. Yet more – perhaps they lunched early – are preparing for a replenishment underway from a Royal Fleet Auxiliary. This starts at 1pm. Today our ship does it by the astern method. At 1.30 we are still exercising replenishment but the communicators are in touch with a naval gunfire support team ashore; and as soon as the oiler is clear, we are off to batter the shoreline with 4.5in gunfire – in a restricted area, of course. This takes us through to 4.30pm, when the navigator is closed up to take the ship through an imaginary, intricate passage into Portland harbour. There most sea riders disembark – but not our libertymen. We are off to sea again for a three-hour anti-submarine exercise; and once the submarine surfaces there are two hours' more drills for the engine room staff. In harbour by 11.30pm, if we are lucky.

Tuesday Leave harbour at 7.45am. Officer of the Watch manoeuvres again, and anti-aircraft weapon direction under the eye of another bunch of sea riders. From 9am to noon, another anti-submarine exercise; we use our helicopter for simulated vectored attacks. At the same time, the weapon sea riders are minutely checking our armament accounts; even the paper has to be right here. Back to harbour at lunchtime, but that's another chimaera; it is just to land a few sea riders, and this time the navigator has to do it blind. Off again for heavy jackstay dummy replenishment with a Dutch support ship. (NATO vessels make much use of Portland and say they greatly benefit. They certainly keep coming back.) Then we do it again, with a light jackstay. At 3.45, having disengaged, we exercise seaboat and swimmer again. But that was just so that others on board could prepare gear to pass again to the Dutchman. This time, we tow him. At 6pm, the tow released, the navigator is at it again on one of his passages through the imaginary narrows. It is dark this time. Then we put to sea and go west of Portland Bill for a night surface action; we have another Dutch ship under command, the opposition is all British. About midnight, back to harbour to land sea riders; but our ship is off again for a long, long anti-submarine exercise, all night in fact. Whoever gets a bit of sleep, it is unlikely to be the captain.

Wednesday Leave harbour (yes, we went in again – at 7am) about 7.30. Officer of the

Aspects of Sea Training at Portland

Below:
Seaboats are exercised whenever opportunity offers.

Below right:
The Navigator pilots the ship through imaginary shoals off the harbour entrance.

Left:
The sea-riding staff transfer by helicopter.

Watch manoeuvres, and anti-aircraft weapon direction with those persistent aircraft of the Fleet Requirements Unit. Today is a gunnery day. We start at 9am with a firing at a towed aircraft target, follow up with an intercept exercise for the benefit of our air direction team, and at 12.15pm the gun's crew and control team try their hand at the more difficult Rushton target. A small diversion when the sea riders play musical chairs by helicopter, then the gun starts blazing away again, this time in surface fire against a target towed by a tug. By the time this is over, it is 4pm. There seems to be time for tea today. But only for some; others are getting ready for the damage control exercise that descends on the ship at 5.30pm. This aims to involve everyone in the ship in some form of damage

Below:
Replenishment at sea for all from the resident 'Rover' class tanker.

Above:
Light anti-aircraft fire, a revived art since the Falklands.

Right:
An exercise in disaster control ashore, done by every ship that passes through.

or nuclear or chemical unpleasantness, and decapitates not a few – all 'for exercise', of course. Once the ship has been made to go again she can enter harbour – by 9pm, with luck, if it is not blowing too hard. (This is January.) The sea riders will want to do a quick post mortem on the damage control exercise, though, before they let you turn in. Every exercise is 'hot washed up' at once, followed by a more considered critique later.

Thursday   Ah, everything before this was peanuts. This is the Thursday War. Our ship is the Commander of a Task Group consisting of six destroyers or frigates, a couple of minesweepers pretending to be something else, and two support ships. We have to get to a position some 30 miles southwest of the Bill, as unscathed as we can in spite of the attentions of opposing submarines, aircraft and surface forces. It is hectic, not least in the operations room. Preparation beforehand will have helped – but when did we find time to do that? As a well-known admiral once said: 'There is always the night'. By 1pm all is over, and the sea riders have told us all our major failings in command and control. Then it's straight into another anti-aircraft firing against a Rushton target, followed by a firing of our lightweight anti-submarine torpedoes by both ship's tubes and helicopter. This is done against a special dummy target and careful records are taken; clever torpedoes must be rigorously tested. Another helicopter transfer of staff, then another fuelling, this time from the Dutch support ship. Again we exercise the seaboat, but this time it's dark. Then the helicopter flies a preset mission, good exercise for it and the direction crews; but for most of the ship a slightly more relaxed evening. After another bout of blind pilotage for the navigator, we are in harbour by midnight.

Friday   Leave harbour at 7.45am, and would you believe Officer of the Watch manoeuvres and an anti-aircraft direction exercise? You would. From 9am to 10.30 there is a main machinery space fire. No, not really, but the realism of the exercise is such that you might be forgiven for thinking so. It is a day for the engineers; the afternoon is taken up with machinery drills. But others will be making up the records, the Flag Officer Sea Training's staff are looking at some of the books. By 3.15pm we are back in harbour; alongside, of all things. Some of us will even get away on weekend leave. We'd better be back on Sunday night though. Next week will be very much like this.

Above:
The proof of the pudding: damage control teams in HMS *Invincible*, 1982.
All Crown Copyright

Left:
Above all, control and co-ordination of effort is a prime product of training. This brilliantly-executed emergency turn to port by a party of flag and senior officers occurred, appropriately, at Portland – when the cap of one of them blew off. *Crown Copyright, photo by the prize-winning Photographic Section, HMS Osprey, 1983*

11 How to be a Medium Maritime Power

Now that Britain's maritime forces and their support and organisation have been described, it is time to revert to the fundamental questions: *What ought they to be able to do? And can they do it?*

To answer the first question properly, it is necessary to make as few assumptions as possible. Far too often strategy as written by politicians and the civil servants who advise them starts halfway down the course, having blandly sidestepped the hurdles of defining vital interests, assessing national strengths and weaknesses, and weighing up both alliances and alliance structures. Having made hidden assumptions on all these matters, such incomplete strategies tend to 'start with the threat' (an old and unimpressive staff college short cut), go on to adumbrate a few secondhand and generalised concepts and take final refuge in a fixed scenario selected to justify the forces in being and planned.

That is not in my view the way to proceed, and within its limitations of space this chapter will attempt to cover the whole course that leads to a sensible view of the maritime side of strategy for this country – however incomplete the detail may be.

There are assumptions that must be made, of course. The first is that Britain is, and means to remain, an individual nation-state. (This is not as obvious as it sounds; many functionaries in Whitehall make the *hidden* assumption that it is no such thing). The second is that Britain will not adopt a force-led or force-directed foreign policy, but neither will it renounce the use or threat of force in circumstances justifiable under the United Nations Charter.

These are not unreasonable assumptions, and for the time being they are the only ones that are required. Next, vital interests must be defined. The most fundamental are suggested by the wording of the United Nations Charter, which prohibits in Article 2(4) the use or threat of force against 'the territorial integrity and political independence' of any state. These are both fully applicable to the United Kingdom. Probably, guarded as she has been by the sea (and her forces in, under and over it), Britain has tended to take her territorial integrity for granted. Troops in South Armagh through the 1970s and 1980s might have something to say about that; and it needs only to be added that as well as the integrity of the land area, that of the zones of the United Kingdom's legitimate offshore interest must be maintained. Nevertheless, it is probably true that political independence is the more jealously guarded of these two vital interests, so far as Britain is concerned. The fear of falling under a foreign tyranny, or a domestic tyranny

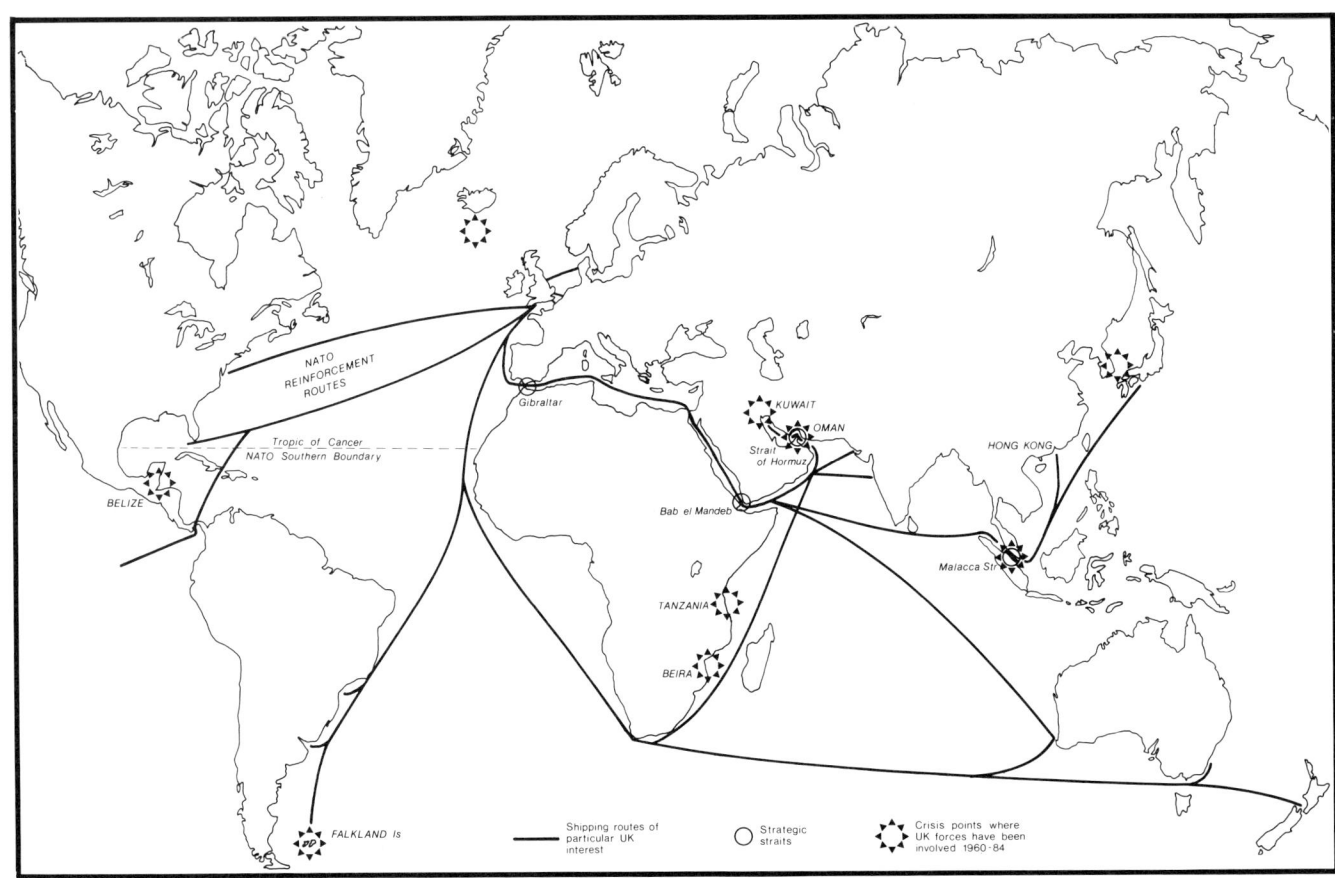

112

Left:
United Kingdom interests and the NATO sea area. *Bob Downey*

Above:
National economic well-being is, for Britain, singularly dependent on the sea. *Crown Copyright*

under foreign influence, is a very strong thread in British history.

But there is much evidence to suggest that territorial integrity and political independence do not exhaust the catalogue of vital interests as perceived in Britain. Well-being is certainly regarded as vital by governments, and it is so regarded because people demand it. If well-being is defined in the broadest possible sense – not only decent food and shelter, but rewarding employment and cultural activity, individual freedom of expression and movement, self-respect – then it probably is the third in a triad of interests that can truly be called vital.

Well-being, though, creates its own web of supporting interests, and it is here that the particular characteristics of Britain need to be assessed. It is an island state to which nearly all goods must come and go by sea. It produces about 70% of its total food consumption. It is self-sufficient in fuel for the next 10 years or so, but over half this fuel comes from offshore workings. It is a manufacturing country with considerable problems of old-fashioned industry and working practices but also considerable potential in new technology. These factors make its exporting and importing patterns, and in particular its

access to overseas markets and to trade routes, unusually important. It is very closely involved with international finance particularly in the fields of trade and insurance. As a post-imperial nation it possesses some clear residues of empire, items of overseas sovereignty which are awkward to keep but shaming to relinquish; and many more tenuous links and interests that can generate both responsibilities and influences. On all these, the national need for self-respect has more to say than might be imagined.

A Medium Maritime Power

Above all, and perhaps summing up this catalogue, Britain is a medium power and a maritime power. She is a medium power because, quite simply, she is neither a superpower – which can safeguard all its vital interests unaided – nor a small power – which cannot unaided protect even its territorial integrity or political independence. Medium powers are quite numerous, but they do not have an easy time. They will always be seeking ways to control their own destiny, simply because they are too large and have too strong a sense of national identity to accept the totally dependent status of a small power; at the same time, they will be conscious that there are in the ultimate some limits to this control because the world has in it two superpowers of global reach.

As for Britain being a maritime power, this goes back to the business of using the sea, the phrase with which this book started. It is clear from every kind of statistic that Britain's use of the sea is very marked. One or two other countries, notably Norway and Japan, may apply proportionately more of their resources to sea use than does Britain; but compared with the

113

vast majority of nations, the United Kingdom is a highly maritime state. This brings both power and dependence. For example, a large merchant marine, such as Britain still has, in spite of recent decline, is an earner of wealth and a safeguard against foreign-flag economic coercion; but it is a vulnerable asset that can be assaulted by nations or groups of individuals.

What, then, are reasonable strategic principles for a state that wishes to control as much as it can of its own destiny and has widespread interests and vulnerabilities of the kind that have been described? It is at this point – and not before – that threats ought to be considered.

Threats

The Soviet Union presents a profound and chronic threat to Britain's political independence, because by its very nature the Soviet dynamic insists that opposing political systems be brought down and replaced by Marxist-Leninist ones. This is held to be the inevitable course of history; but every loyal Communist must give it a push. It is also a threat to Britain's well-being; clearly to the freedoms such well-being implies, but also economically, since the Soviet Union could tolerate in the long run no country more prosperous than itself, however ruled.

The threat is chronic rather than acute, partly because the USSR thinks time is on its side and the 'correlation of forces' moving in its direction, and partly because it is inhibited from overt military action by the deterrent structure of the West. Nevertheless a great deal of the dynamic of the threat is military in character. Up to about 1965 this was overwhelmingly on land and predominantly on the Central Front in Germany. Since then it has steadily become more widespread and diverse and included deployed sea forces of an increasingly powerful and balanced nature. There have been numerous sea-based initiatives such as the Mediterranean reinforcements in recurring crises, the Indian Ocean reactions during the Indo-Pakistan war of 1971, and world-wide exercises at five-year intervals; and many more maritime operations in support of land initiatives, notably in Africa. None of this has led to conflict and not all has resulted in the strengthening of the Soviet position; the ratchet sometimes slips. But nowhere in the world can it now be *guaranteed* that the Soviet Navy will not intervene in tension or crisis; that is a measure of the way the threat has changed, and to a maritime power with world-wide interests this is of great significance.

The strength of the Soviet Navy is well documented and only the broadest indication need be given here. The emphasis is on submarines, of which there are over 300, more than half nuclear-powered and many armed with tactical missiles mainly for anti-ship purposes and with ranges of several hundred miles. There are several hundred long-range tactical strike aircraft, also missile-armed, and heavily armed surface units including four aircraft carriers and numerous cruiser-sized vessels for both surface and anti-submarine warfare. Increasing provision is made for amphibious warfare and replenishment at sea.

Against such a force, or even the Northern Fleet component of it, no maritime forces available from Britain's resources could sustain a conflict alone. Thus, even when judged in the solely maritime context, allies against a Soviet threat are ultimately necessary. This simply reinforces a view which can be derived from Britain's strong economic, cultural and political links with Europe and the USA, and the Soviet land and air threat to them: that an alliance comprehending Western Europe, and implicating the USA in its defence, must be a key element in British strategy.

Yet there are other threats which, while less weighty, may be more acute. The Falklands was an extreme example (and one which, it is fair to say, was regularly smiled out of consideration by civilian and Foreign Office planners throughout the 1970s); but from incidents of piracy up through the gamut of cod wars and confrontations, to say nothing of the incidents that did not develop because of the timely deterrent deployments of maritime forces, there have been enough concerning the British Navy alone, over the past 20 years, to make it possible to say to sceptics: 'You have a 100% failure rate so far; how can you say it will not happen again?'

The size and shape of such threats will range from medium-power maritime forces to small armed bands. The sort of forces deployed by Argentina – one carrier, four submarines, a dozen frigates – are not untypical, and the Falklands conflict demonstrated the unpleasant truth that an opponent may often be able to call on shore-based resources in the maritime role. One further significant element of the typical threat, which was not in evidence in the South Atlantic, is the missile-armed coastal or offshore craft. These are nowadays by no means confined, as they used to be, to Soviet clients.

But what are these threats to? Do they matter? Yes, they do. They are threats to stability and confidence, to the rule of law at sea, to orderly access to routes and markets. One such threat, in isolation, may not appear vital; many, accumulated, clearly are. Yet, unhappily, memories are short, and they are even shorter in continental Europe than in Britain; the perception of such threats' implications is often confined to Britain alone, and sometimes to small sections of British opinion. Moreover, and perhaps more critically, they are not always apparent to the USA, a country less dependent on the sea economically than its maritime deployments – which are largely for purposes of power projection and not trade protection – suggest.

Britain then has something of a dilemma. Compelled to a European-American alliance because of the massive, latent Soviet threat, she has nevertheless interests which are more sensitive than those of her allies to other threats, less in scale but often more acute. The position is not helped by the fact that NATO, the Western alliance as it is, is continental in posture, geographically restricted, and highly structured.

Some Helpful Tools

To lift Britain off the horns of this dilemma and arrive at a sensible maritime force structure, there are some useful tools. These are, on the whole, conceptual rather than technical; there is no universal ray-gun that makes everything different in the twinkling of a maritime eye; the laws of physics are not like that. The tools that may help here are the notions of deterrence, levels of conflict, and reach.

Deterrence

The essence of deterrence is to convince an opponent that no military action on his part will end profitably for him. At its upper limit, deterrence means confronting the opponent with the certainty that should he launch a massive onslaught on you,

Right:
Aspects of the Soviet threat: the missile armed battlecruiser *Kirov* and 'Victor' class nuclear submarine.

Above:

Normal conditions: but in peace, maritime forces must be ready and sufficient to face an emergency. *Crown Copyright*

Below:

Deterrence: a Polaris submarine represents the highest level only; there are many other aspects.

he will suffer unacceptable damage. Against a very large, powerful opponent that almost certainly means nuclear weapons. But lower down the scale deterrence can quite simply mean the ability to react with sufficient force to blunt an assault, to buy time for reinforcements to arrive or for a politically ambivalent situation to develop; while at the very bottom end it may just mean the ability to create a politico-military fuss. At these lower grades of deterrence, though, there is a proviso: there must be some ability to drive the situation into a more severe form. This is called variously escalation or flexible response.

Levels of Conflict

It has already been suggested that deterrence is a staged process. Conflict – which by one definition is the breakdown of deterrence – is also definable by stages or levels. The lowest we may call normal conditions: deterrence is operating in a routine way; military forces are occupied in training, peaceable deployments and visits; normal surveillance of potential enemies is conducted; offshore regulation is at the level necessary for good order. The watchwords are readiness and sufficiency. The next level is low intensity operations: these never merit the title of war, are limited in aim, scope and area, and are generally governed by the international law of self-defence under strict rules of engagement. There is much premium in not firing the first shot. Typically they are demonstrations of right or resolve, the passage of reinforcements in time of tension, evacuation of civilians, anti-gunrunning. The watchword is precision; weapon systems must be discriminating and flexible, communications excellent, public image appropriately presented. The next grade is operations at the higher level: these are active hostilities involving on both sides fleet units and aircraft, with the use of major weapons. There may still be limits both geographical and in terms of rules of engagement, particularly over nuclear weapons on which political control will be absolute. But there will be ample scope for all other kinds of weapon system, including the heavier and less discriminating ones. The final level is general war; this by definition involves both major alliances and carries the risk, though not the absolute certainty, of escalation to nuclear levels at some stage.

Reach

This can be defined as the distance from the home base at which operations (of a given level) can be sustained. Up to the late 1960s Britain could with some justification claim that her

Aspects of Surveillance

Top:
Outside the NATO area, a look at the Soviet amphibious vessel *Ivan Rogov*. *Crown Copyright*

Above:
In the NATO area, a Nimrod 3 airborne early warning aircraft of the RAF. *Crown Copyright*

maritime reach for higher level operations was not just world-wide but global. This was ensured not only by the lower calibre of likely opposition then, but by the possession of large advanced bases and of ship-based striking power from both aircraft and amphibious troops. By 1982 reach had been severely eroded by the insistence of successive governments on NATO criteria, with the imposed limit of the Tropic of Cancer as a southern boundary which that implied; and even with exceptional efforts of improvisation it was only just

sufficient to do the job in the South Atlantic, against another medium power, in what was undoubtedly an operation at the higher level.

A Pattern for British Strategy

How do these tools help to shape a pattern for British strategy in the 1980s? It seems to me that they can do so in the following way, observing first that it is the national interest that must be safeguarded; there is no room for altruism here, if being a nation-state means anything. The NATO alliance is necessary, since it is the only one to which Britain can reasonably turn; but Britain's interests are not coincident with NATO's (if indeed there are such things as 'NATO interests'). She must, therefore, be capable of doing certain things on her own; and this, not a 'contribution to the alliance', must be the measure of her force requirements.

Here the notions of deterrence, levels of conflict and reach all come to our aid. First, deterrence: it is worthwhile (considering that we already possess nuclear weapons and the capacity to make more) to have a strategic nuclear deterrent to safeguard Britain, in the ultimate, from selective nuclear attack. But it must, credibly, threaten unacceptable damage to the Soviet Union; if it does not do that, it is worth little in the Soviet context, though it would still be valuable in the event of nuclear proliferation; and, if it costs so much as to weaken all other levels of deterrence to the point of incredibility, it is not worth while.

So we begin to establish our limits. Second, levels of conflict: it is inconceivable that we could sustain a higher-level conflict indefinitely against the Soviet Union at sea. But we might conceivably need to take the brunt of a first assault, and then re-enter the conflict, in order to demonstrate to our allies – and particularly the United States – our determination not to give in, and thereby convince them that they must intervene. Against threats other than from the Soviet Union, it is far more likely that we should be on our own throughout, with no more than moral or at most logistic support from allies, so that ability independently to bring a higher level maritime conflict to a successful conclusion against another medium power is required. Both the Soviet and non-Soviet cases can be used to define force limits. Scenarios can be used to test the force structures that are derived – but must not be used to guarantee them.

Finally, reach: after the Falklands, who can say that in the ultimate this can be anything but world-wide? Naturally resources will not allow forces able to fight a higher-level conflict to be 'on the spot on the dot'; but naval forces have the great advantage of being mobile, and can use that quality to mount a higher-level capability world-wide – which is implicit in the whole threat assessment and strategy outlined above.

This all sounds too tidy and clearcut by half, and so it is: first, because the world is an untidy place and geographical, political and military factors may make successful operations inconceivable in some circumstances; and second, because any alliance is bound to exact some price in the form of special force structures and deployments from each of its participants, and so Britain's membership of NATO must be taken into account – which is not the same as to say that it must govern her maritime provision.

Measuring Up

How then do Britain's maritime forces – the military arm of our ability to use the sea – measure up to the requirements of the strategy outlined above? It is as well to examine them

Above:
Cheerful co-operation ashore, as afloat; but are NATO criteria enough to govern the requirement for UK maritime forces?
Crown Copyright

Right:
Three styles of offshore patrol vessel: from top, 'Castle', 'Island' and 'Ton' classes. *Crown Copyright. Flag Officer Scotland & Northern Ireland's photographic section.*

under the headings of the levels of conflict, since these throw up more distinctive force requirements than the other parameters.

Normal Conditions

The first watchword is readiness. British maritime forces are probably better trained than any in the world: all-volunteer, and with up to now a sound career structure properly rewarding experience and performance, they are of proved worth. But all this could be eroded by too severe a cut in manpower or too swift and disruptive a change in training patterns. Exercises are the far end of training; and both inter-service and allied exercises are needed as well as within-service ones. These are adequate at present. There have been periods when Treasury-imposed budgetary cuts have imposed a logistic moratorium that disrupted exercise patterns; these are damaging and must be avoided by a less rigid insistence on year-on-year budgeting.

The second watchword is sufficiency. In this section let us – while observing the daunting effect on an aggressor of forces that are capable right through the gamut of conflict – confine ourselves to three aspects in which forces must clearly be sufficient in normal conditions: surveillance, the regulation of offshore waters, and strategic deterrence.

Surveillance assets include shore-based Nimrod 2 aircraft and Nimrod 3 airborne early warning aircraft; shipborne anti-submarine and, now, airborne early warning helicopters.

With other forms of aircraft including Sea Harriers, these can mount surface searches as well. Ships can conduct surveillance when high visibility is no worry and good endurance is needed, while submarines are excellent covert surveillance vehicles when no immediate, real-time reporting (which would expose them to detection) is needed. Recalling the definition of normal conditions, and remembering too the intelligence back-up that exists, Britain's surveillance assets in the Eastern Atlantic and Channel areas are just about adequate, though tracking even a single submarine by aircraft for any length of time does eat into the aircraft hours and sonobuoy stocks. Outside the NATO area, given the lack of shore bases for large aircraft, surveillance resources are ship-based and severely stretched. More AEW helicopters are needed; that means less deck space for ASW helicopters; that means more deck space generally, perhaps in Arapaho ships, is desirable.

Offshore regulation is a growing activity, with a squadron now nearly 20 ships strong as well as air and Royal Marines assets. But with wider limits and powers over increasing sea use, the task grows too. Britain keeps pace pretty well with her relatively modern force, reasonably well matched now to the task, although in the air the Nimrods are more sophisticated and expensive than is needed for offshore work.

Finally, providing a sufficient strategic deterrent is bound to present particularly acute problems for a medium power. 'Unacceptable damage' is a difficult criterion; the nation-state to be deterred is not likely to tell you what it would find unacceptable. There is no doubt that successive governments have founded their force requirements on as careful an assessment as they could make, and that both Polaris/Chevaline and Trident are calculated to give the Soviet Union the certainty that it would suffer unacceptable damage (to 'the centres of Soviet state power', as the official document has it) if they were used, even though all Soviet resources were deployed against them. The number of submarines is small – four Polaris followed by four Trident – and the margins are not inherently wide; but there is evidence both from experience up to now, and from the future course of anti-submarine and anti-missile technology, that they are wide enough. That the cost of this strategic force should be borne by naval budgets is, to many including myself, a nonsense.

Low Intensity Operations
There are two basic kinds of low intensity operations: those concerned with sea use and those concerned with sea denial. They can of course also be qualified by reach – those that take place away from home impose quite different requirements from those taking place in home waters.

Sea use operations often involve some demonstration of right or resolve; Being There is often sufficient. But to exercise the right sort of deterrence, weapons of some variety and scope are needed, there must be good communication and the image

must be right – low intensity operations are almost always politico-military in nature. Typically, the frigate is the protagonist; a ship with plenty of visibility, not too overbearing a presence, sufficient power to put up a fight. Britain has a fair spread of frigates, from the Type 22s with their fine self-defence weapons but perhaps too little flexibility in surface action and very high material and manpower investment, to the Type 21s which some consider too flimsy although they have a very fair spread of weapons for operations of this type. If this writer may put up a rather heretical view, he would not put too great an emphasis on the ability to look after oneself in this sort of operation. A single ship can almost always be overwhelmed, however good its defensive systems. Numbers are likely to be more important than single-ship quality. If 10% extra capability means 50%

extra cost – and at the top end of the cost-effectiveness scale that is not unusual – it should be foregone in favour of more ships. So the Type 23, and perhaps cheaper units still, must be the way to go to optimise for operations of this sort. And indeed, this must a fortiori be the case for sea denial operations such as anti-gunrunning or anti-piracy patrols. Numbers matter greatly here, quality nothing like so much – so long as there are certain basic characteristics, such as helicopters to extend surveillance range and a decent spread of surface weapons. Britain's capacity for this sort of task is eroded by the diminishing number of frigates and the over-specialisation of some; it may cope with most contingencies but ought to be better.

Other units – submarines, large surface ships and fixed-wing aircraft – may have a place in low-intensity operations, but not

Frigates and Destroyers, Key Units in Low Intensity Operations

Above:
HMS *Brazen*.

Right:
HMS *Charybdis*. Too high a quality for the job?
All Crown Copyright

Far right:
HMS *Glasgow*.

usually in the forefront of the action. They provide the necessary backing in case reinforcement or escalation are required; they may also be important in the surveillance role. Good communications and control are essential, and submarines in particular are not always easy to handle in these matters. The British maritime forces are adequately equipped to provide the backing, so long as three carriers – one up and one back and one in dockyard hands, in the worst case – are retained in service.

Amphibious deployments as an element of low intensity operations are still a possible requirement; consider, for example, the deterrent effect of landing a Commando in a friendly country to forestall aggression. Here the British ability to conduct an administrative landing, given enough warning, is still adequate; but the loss of troop-carrying flat-topped ships

Above:

Much reliance – arguably too much? – is now placed on 'intelligent' torpedoes for anti-submarine work.
Marconi Underwater Systems Ltd

makes so-called 'vertical envelopment' by helicopter a most unlikely business now, though it could just be done on a small scale by the 'Invincible' class.

Reach for low intensity operations, as provided by the RFA (STUFT would scarcely be allowed), is probably adequate. The ability to support a peacetime round-the-world deployment is evidence enough of sufficiency here.

Higher Level Operations
If such operations develop from conditions of low intensity, the transition may well be a traumatic one involving – as has already been observed – casualties to men and probably to ships too. The ability to move swiftly to a more general use of weapons, probably in a wider area or at least over longer ranges, is a function as much of command and control as of weapon quality and numbers.

Command and control the British forces have. The communications equipment may not be the most modern in the world but it has kept abreast of the latest techniques and proved adequate in the Falklands – for everyone except the Press, at least. Weapons and outfits are more controversial.

Surface ships in general have rather few channels of anti-aircraft and anti-missile fire. Their ability to engage multiple targets depends critically on everything working to its design limits, and we know that all too often those limits are not achieved. There is a need for more and simpler air defence systems – even of the strap-on sort. Again, some ships over-specialised in ASW are quite inadequately supplied with air defence.

So far as ASW itself is concerned, it seems likely that too much money has been spent on straining after high quality in

Left:
HMS *Invincible*, happily still one of a class of three, and fitted with additional close range weapons. *Crown Copyright*

Above:
Airborne Early Warning Sea King helicopter with parent Gannet in attendance. *Crown Copyright*

Below:
The fleet submarine HMS *Tireless* at her launch.
Vickers Shipbuilders Ltd

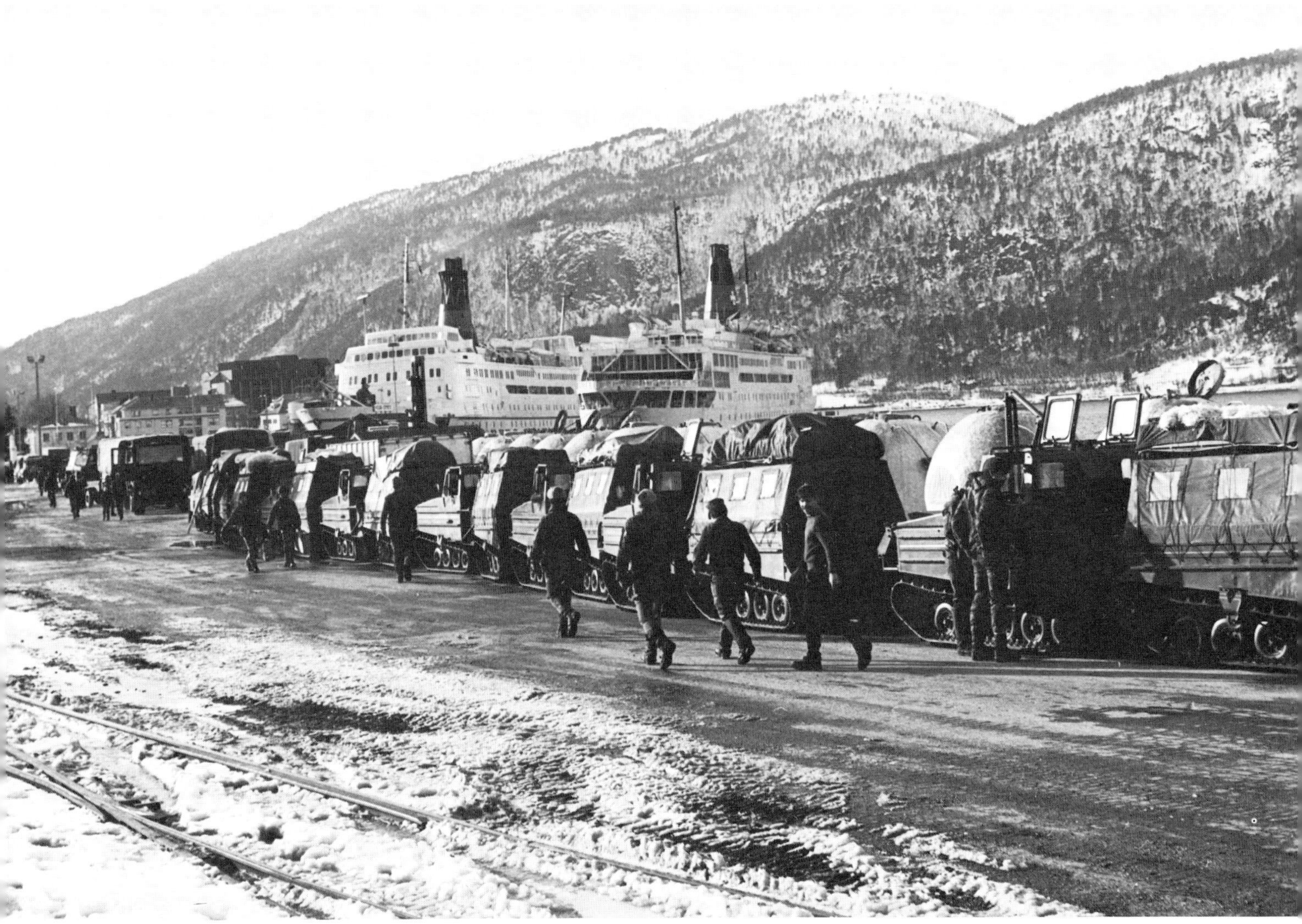

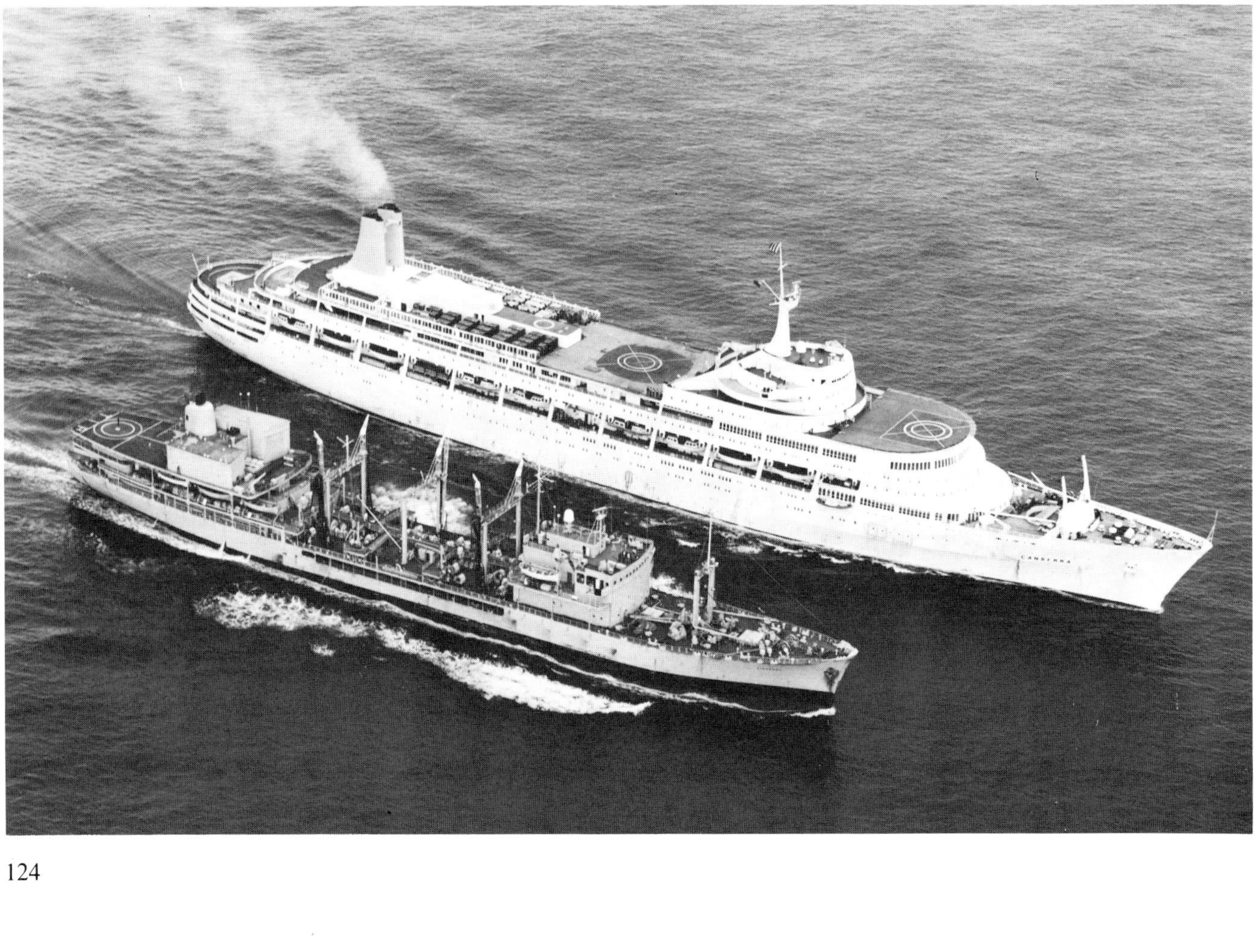

Above left:
Awaiting embarkation at Aandalsnes, a queue of Royal Marines vehicles suggests some of the limitations of improvised amphibious shipping. *Crown Copyright*

Left:
A strong merchant marine is necessary to provide ships to be taken up from trade in emergency: *Canberra* **during the Falklands campaign.** *Crown Copyright*

Above:
British ships are equipped and trained for decontamination after being subjected to nuclear fallout or chemical attack.
Crown Copyright

hull-mounted sonars. The ability to counter-attack – the most likely use of such a sonar – depends much more on water conditions, standards of training and how the opposing submarine is handled, than on a 10% increment in sonar range or even classification ability. Towed arrays, on the other hand, are worth investment since they are far down the learning curve. ASW weapons concentrate too much on the 'clever' torpedo; the torpedo's record, at the start of wars, is unimpressive; something cruder is likely to be needed to keep enemy heads down. Nevertheless, surface ships would probably exact a higher toll of submarines in the open ocean than the pessimists expect.

Surface-to-surface warfare is likely to be as much a matter of tactics as weapon range. Most British ships now have Exocet and it is a proven weapon, as everyone knows.

Harpoon, to be fitted in the next generation, is well proved too, and of longer range.

Maritime aircraft too have of course a large part to play in anti-surface vessel warfare, and the British will be better provided in this field when they get the Sea Eagle missile. But the main aircraft function is in ASW, and here we find a lot of systems unproven in war. Torpedoes have already been mentioned. Sonobuoys – provided stocks hold out – are generally pretty reliable, certainly so long as the target submarine co-operates by making a noise or has the tactical necessity of making a noise imposed upon it by our own dispositions. Helicopter-borne active sonar is no wasting asset when submarine quietening is so fashionable. The real problem in airborne ASW is numbers: you can never have enough, and must make maximum tactical use of every asset you have. But with 10 squadrons of ASW aircraft (not counting Lynxes and Wasps) Britain certainly mounts a strong air ASW effort, probably the second most powerful in the world.

British submarines are vastly capable in the anti-ship role. This assessment is not just an extrapolation from the *Belgrano* affair, but is drawn from knowledge of the qualities of the boats and their crews, and experience in exercises. It is certain that the British nuclear submarine force is a serious consideration even for the Soviet surface fleet, and a terror to those of other medium powers. In the submarine-versus-submarine role the situation is less certain. The fact is that it has never been tried in war, depends on a multitude of factors any one of which could be critical, and uses weapons that have gone through a lot of teething troubles. My own assessment, and my submariner friends will not thank me for it, is that the rates of successful engagement would be a good deal lower in war than might have been expected from the publicity given to the submarine as 'clearly the best anti-submarine vehicle'.

All in all, British maritime forces can be said to have been optimised for operations at the higher level, and in the NATO area contain all the necessary elements for such operations. There, the questions concern the balance for the tasks that have been allocated, and numbers within that balance. When one considers the threat from submarines against both the strike fleet and reinforcement shipping, it is clear that defence in depth, not reliance on linear barriers, is by far the most sensible counter, and that tactical manoeuvre, well-planned to impose the maximum exposure on submarines, is an important adjunct. (This philosophy is explained at more length in the writer's *Anti-Submarine Warfare*, published by Ian Allan Ltd.) In consequence, the unbalancing of British maritime forces away from surface ships is serious and ought to be corrected. Air defence is a matter for the Navy itself to correct; more channels of fire, from simpler systems, are required.

These considerations apply very largely to higher-level operations in the national interest, against other medium powers. The threat from submarines in such operations is not so severe as that from the Russians, but the penalties of failure to counter it would be just as high and no Nimrods might be available. Thus the Navy needs good ASW, and in depth out to at least 100 miles from the force centre. It also needs good anti-surface capability; but that it has, and to a sufficient range so long as the VSTOL aircraft force is kept up to date. Most of all, though, it needs good air defence; and here, although eschewing any sort of no-casualties policy, one must reiterate that every sort of device from air defence VSTOL aircraft through hard-kill ship-mounted weapons to chaff dispensers must be vigorously sought and deployed – with the proviso that

impossibly high kill rates should give place in the staff requirements to simplicity, ease of fitting and multiple channels of fire. Every element of command, control and information was tested in the Falklands; most passed the test but some, notably of course AEW, were deficient. They have been put right, but at a price in deck space; that ought to be retrieved, and one *Reliant* is probably not enough. News in Spring 1984 that the *Contender Bezant* had been bought for a similar conversion was, therefore, very welcome. Finally, the requirements of reach were triumphantly met by the RFA and STUFT, and – given a surviving merchant fleet, which urgently needs government attention – could be met again.

I notice that nowhere in this account of higher level operations have I mentioned amphibious forces. This is perhaps because I have so much faith in the survival of the Royal Marines. But – as already indicated – their capacity for helicopter-borne assault, certainly at Commando strength, is largely eroded, and the question is whether it should be restored. This is an extremely difficult matter, for it would require heavy expenditure on a specialised ship or ships for a relatively narrow range of tasks, all of which could be done – though less certainly and smoothly – in other ways. Perhaps our old friend Arapaho is the key to the answer here too.

One further problem at the higher level that seems particularly intractable for Britain is that of countering extensive mine warfare. Mineable waters round Britain are so extensive, and Soviet mine stocks so large, that keeping all ports and channels open would demand a vastly expensive effort. The new impetus, with three classes of mine countermeasures vessel, represents the operational minimum – and probably the economic maximum too: the retired 'Ton' class should not be thrown away but kept in reserve.

General War

That one short paragraph only should be devoted to general war is partly an earnest of one's hope that it will never come to that; but also it implies that nearly all the ground has been covered in previous sections. 'Defence' against tactical nuclear weapons is partly a matter of meeting them beyond their lethal range (Sea Dart and Sea Wolf are the best hopes here) and partly of avoiding fallout areas and applying decontamination measures. British ships are well equipped for this aspect of operations.

The Reckoning

Maritime forces are not instantly realisable in a flash of creative lightning. They have grown, and decayed, through the previous 30 years or so in material terms, through much longer ages sometimes in terms of tradition, morale and training. It would be entirely understandable therefore if British maritime forces did not measure up to the tasks they are now likely to be called upon to do – particularly since, as we have seen, some of those tasks are not acknowledged by the powers that be in spite of all the evidence.

The analysis in this chapter suggests that at present most contingencies threatening the country's vital interests at sea could be met satisfactorily by the maritime forces in their state of post-Falklands boost. It is far less certain that in five years' time, with the partial reversion at present in progress to the pale strategy and false tactical appreciations of the 1981 review, that assessment will still hold. Near-run things are a traditional British habit of warfare, and the Falklands success is clearly a helpful deterrent to other powers contemplating an adventure against British interests; but you cannot live on reputation for ever. Enough money must be provided to keep up numbers and the minimum capabilities that have been described.

But things happen in strange ways in the machinery of defence, and some optimism is justified. After all, over the last decade and a half, faced with the artificial horizons of the Eastern Atlantic and the 'contribution' strategy, the Navy managed to retain ship-based fixed-wing combat aircraft; high-grade anti-submarine helicopters and the ships to carry them; a satellite communication system of world-wide scope; a Fleet Auxiliary of nearly 30 ships giving wide logistic autonomy; and a force of fleet submarines that makes it unquestionably the third most powerful navy in the world. The maritime side of the Royal Air Force, not its most glamorous arm, remained viable, indeed was strengthened. And exceptionally high standards of training were maintained. This has been achieved by the tenacity of all the people of the services concerned, but particularly those in the Ministry of Defence who are often so much maligned. They may not have got everything right, and they may have felt their way instinctively rather than articulated their ideas; but they got it a great deal more right than the politicians, the pundits and the press, and proved it in 1982. Without sea power, that year would have been one of great shame. We should all do well not to forget it.

The Greatest Single Factor

Highly-trained, well-motivated people are still the core value of maritime fighting forces. *Crown Copyright*

Bibliography

To some extent all the sources for *The Royal Navy Today and Tomorrow*, acknowledged on page 143 of that book, are valid for this one. If I pick out some of them now, it is because they stick in the memory as having been particularly influential. On history the core works include Peter Kemp's edition of many contributors in *The History of the Royal Navy* (Barker, 1969); Marder's *From the Dreadnought to Scapa Flow* (OUP, 1961); Roskill's *The War at Sea* (HMSO, 1953); and Chatfield's *The Navy and Defence* (Heinemann, 1943). On the task and on medium maritime power, Cable's *Gunboat Diplomacy* and *Britain's Naval Future* (Macmillan, 1982 and 1983) vied with Gorshkov's *The Sea Power of the State* (Pergamon Press, 1978) as leading marks. Till's *Maritime Strategy in the Nuclear Age* and (with Ranft) his *The Sea in Soviet Strategy* (Macmillan, 1981 and 1983) are important new works, and O'Connell's *The Influence of Law on Sea Power* (Manchester UP, 1975) still has much to say.

For the other, more factual chapters (3-10 inclusive), the sources were more diffuse. Pride of place must go to official documents: the Statements on the Defence Estimates (which of course were also useful in expounding the official version of the maritime task); the Directorate of Public Relations (Navy) with its descriptive leaflets of ship classes and its excellent summary of developments in the annual Broadsheet; the recruiting literature, which gives much more than information on career patterns and entry standards, and sponsors an excellent leaflet on *The Royal Navy: Ships, Aircraft and Missiles*; government documents on defence, particularly the White Papers *Defence: The Way Forward* (Cmnd 8288) and *The Falklands Campaign: The Lessons* (Cmnd 8758), and Open Government Document 80/23, *The Future UK Strategic Deterrent Force*; and parliamentary debates in Hansard.

Many of the hard facts, dimensions and numbers, appeared in these sources. But there was always a useful check, and often more information, in the non-official literature. Of the books, the Jane's series was as ever the most comprehensive; much of the information in the tables is derived from that excellent source. *The Military Balance* produced annually by the International Institute for Strategic Studies was also indispensable, as in a quite different way was a splendid little paperback on helicopters called *Flashing Blades over the Sea*, by J. M. Milne (Maritime Books, 1979). I also had recourse to manufacturers' literature; a tour round the stalls at the Royal Navy Equipment Exhibition was most productive.

Promotion leaflets, too, were a good guide to all that could properly be said about the way various weapons and equipments work. Articles in the technical literature, particularly the *International Defence Review*, *Naval Forces*, *Military Technology*, *NATO's Sixteen Nations* and *Navy International* often filled out the basic facts in the brochures. On the difficult subject of sonar, Tsipis' work in *The Future of the Sea-Based Deterrent* (MIT Press, 1973) and Urick's *Sound Propagation in the Sea* (DARPA, 1979) were the best reading for the non-technical eye.

Finally I must pay tribute to two magazines that do not pretend to be technical journals but pack more hard professional news into their entertaining pages than many glossier publications. These are the Royal Marines' bi-monthly *Glove and Laurel* – after reading its 1982 editions there was no need to read books on the Royal Marines' participation in the Falklands campaign – and the monthly *Navy News*. This remarkable paper, regarded as totally approachable and readable by every rank of the Navy, manages for all its liveliness and appeal to give up-to-date and accurate news on everything related to the Service including reorganisation at the most elevated levels in the Ministry of Defence. It will probably be my principal source for updating between manuscript and galley-proof stage, and justifiably so.